Discordia

HAIL ERIS GODDESS OF CHAOS AND CONFUSION

The Magnum Opiate of Malaclypse the Younger
& Lord Omar Khayyam Ravenhurst

RONIN
Berkeley, CA
www.roninpub.com

HAIL ERIS
ALL HAIL DISCORDIA
POEE

Discordia

INTRODUCTION TO
THE ERISIAN MYSTEREEE

as Divinely Revealed to
My High Reverence
MALACLYPSE THE YOUNGER, KSC
Omnibenevolent Polyfather of Virginity in Gold
HIGH PRIEST of
THE PARATHEO-ANAMETAMYSTIKHOOD
OF ERIS ESOTERIC
(POEE)

HAIL ERIS!

✦ καλλιχτι ✦

ALL HAIL DISCORDIA
DISCORDIAN SOCIETY

Discordia: Hail Eris Goddess of Chaos & Confusion
Copyright 2006 by Ronin Publishing, Inc.
ISBN: 1-57951-029-9; 978-1-157951-029-9
Published by
Ronin Publishing, Inc.
PO Box 22900
Oakland, CA 94609
www.roninpub.com

Editor:	Beverly A. Potter	docpotter.com
Interior Design:	Beverly A. Potter	
Cover Design:	Brian Groppe	briangroppe.com

Fonts: Adobe: Madrone, ParkAve. Apple: Spumoni, Symbol, TimesRoman. Astigmatic: ComicFX, MardiParty, Ocovilla, Spruce. Bigelow & Holmes Type: LucidaBlackletter, Wingdings. Braineaters: ChannelTuning. Buttfaces: GrumpyButt. Chank: Blockobat, Challoops, CouchLover, MisterKrisky, PlayerPiano, Sauertwiggo, UncleStinky, Venis, Westsec. Digital Font Data: DesignerTillingCaps. Font Head: Bonkers, Butterfingers, CircusDog, DanceParty, Holstein, JohnDoe, Keener, Mondo,Pesto, Smock, SpaceCowBoy, Submarine. John Martz: ScienceProject. Microsoft: Trebuchet. Nerfect Type: CrapMagnet, SpeedDemon. Nick Curtis: RubarbPie. PizzaDude: Malapropism. Ray Larabie: GlazKrak, Mufferaw, SendCash, TopBond, Vademecum. Robotic Attack Fonts: GirlsAreWeird. Swifte Intern'l: Raskin. Tailspin Studio: Stuph. Typedelic Fonts: StoneHinge. WSI Fonts: Drop Caps.

Library of Congress Card Number: 2006901954
Distributed to the book trade by **Publishers Group West**
Printed in the United States by **United Graphics**

DISCORDIAN SOCIETY

Committed to an advanced
understanding of the Paraphysical
manifestations of everyday chaos

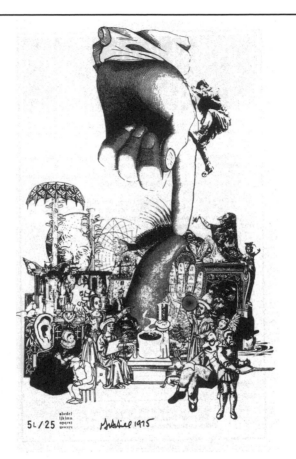

5L/25   abcdef ijklmn opqrst uvwxyz   Grabiel 1975

Absolutely Everything Worth Knowing
About Absolutely Nothing

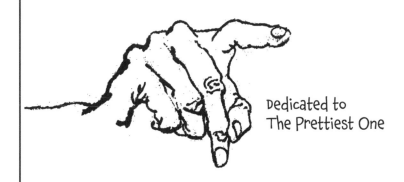

Dedicated to
The Prettiest One

THE UPROAR OF ONE HAND CLAPPING.

I TELL YOU: ONE MUST STILL HAVE CHAOS IN ONE TO GIVE BIRTH TO A DANCING STAR!
—Nietzsche

THE SACRED

ΚΑΛΛΙΣΤΙ

CHAO

Table of Contents

Table of Contents continued

Table of Contents continued

Chaos

Chaos is the nothingness out of which the first objects of existence appeared. These first beings, described as children of Chaos were:

Gaia – the Earth,
Tartarus – the Underworld,
Eros – desire,
Nyx – the darkness of the night, and
Erebus – the darkness of the Underworld.

The deities related to each element known to man, beginning with the primordial elements: the Earth, the starry Sky, the Sea.

According to Hesiod's
Theogonia

THE BIRTH OF THE ERISIAN MOVEMENT

THE REVELATION

Just prior to the decade of the ninteen-sixties, when Sputnik was alone and new, and about the time that Ken Kesey took his first acid trip as a medical volunteer; before underground newspapers, Viet Nam, and talk of a second American Revolution; in the comparative quiet of the late nineteen-fifties, just before the idea of RENAISSANCE became relevant . . .

FIRST I MUST SPRINKLE YOU
WITH FAIRY DUST

Two young Californians, known later as Omar Ravenhurst and Malaclypse the Younger, were indulging in their habit of sipping coffee at an all night bowling alley and generally solving the world's problems.

014

This particular evening the main subject of discussion was discord and they were complaining to each other of the personal confusion they felt in their respective lives. "Solve the problem of discord," said one, "and all other problems will vanish." "Indeed," said the other, "chaos and strife are the roots of all confusion."

Suddenly—
   The place became devoid of light.
Then an utter silence enveloped them,
and a great stillness was felt.

   There came a blinding flash of intense
light, as though their very psyches had gone
nova.

   Then vision returned.

I hear music!

015

The two were dazed and neither moved nor spoke for several minutes. They looked around and saw that the bowlers were frozen like statues in a variety of comic positions, and that a bowling ball was steadfastedly anchored to the floor only inches from the pins that it had been sent to scatter.

The two looked at each other, totally unable to account for phenomenon. The condition was one of suspension and energy. The clock had stopped.

There walked into the room a shaggy monkey all grey about the mussle, yet upright to his full height, and poised with natural majesty. He carried a scroll and walked over to the young men.

10. The Earth quakes and the Heavens rattle; the beasts of nature flock together and the nations of men flock apart; volcanoes usher up heat while elsewhere water becomes ice and melts; and then on other days it just rains. 11. Indeed do many things come to pass.

HBT: The Book of Predications, Chap. 19

016

"Gentlemen.," he said, "why does Pickering's Moon go about in reverse orbit? Gentlemen, there are nipples on your chests; do you give milk? And what, pray tell, Gentlemen, is to be done about Heisenberg's Law?"

He paused. "SOMEBODY HAD TO HAVE PUT ALL OF THIS CONFUSION HERE!"

And with that he revealed his scroll. It was a diagram, like a yin-yang with a

Pentagon

Apple

pentagon on one side and an apple on the other. Then he exploded and the two lost consciousness.

ΚΑΛΛΙΣΤΙ

They awoke to the sound of pins clattering, and found the bowlers engaged in their game and the waitress busy with making coffee. It was apparant that their experience had been private.

They discussed their strange encounter and reconstructed from memory the monkey's diagram. Over the next five days they searched libraries to find the significance of it, but were disappointed to uncover only references to Taoism, the Korean flag, and Technocracy.

018

◻19

It was not until they traced the Greek writing on the apple that they discovered the ancient Goddess known to the Greeks as ERIS and to the Romans as DISCORDIA. This was on the fifth night, and when they slept that night each had a vivid dream of a splendid woman whose eyes were as soft as feather and as deep as eternity itself, and whose body was the spectacular dance of atoms and universes. Pyrotechnics of pure energy formed her flowing hair, and rainbows manifested and dissolved as she spoke in a warm and gentle voice:

They dreamed of ERIS. I don't know if it was wet.

ENTER ERIS:

GODDESS OF CHAOS,

DISCORD

& CONFUSION

020

SOME KNOW ME AS CAT WOMAN!

I have come to tell you that **you are free.**
Many ages ago, my consciousness left man, that
he might develop himself. I return to find this
development approaching completion, but
hindered by fear and by misunderstanding.

You have built for yourselves psychic suits
of armor, and clad in them, your vision is
restricted, your movements are clumsy and
painful, your skin is bruised, and your spirit
is broiled in the sun.

I am chaos. I am the substance from which
your artists and scientists build rhythms. I am
the spirit with which your children and clowns
laugh in happy anarchy. I am chaos. I am alive,
and I tell you that you are free.

During the next months they studied philosophies and theologies, and learned that **ERIS** or **DISCORDIA** was primarily feared by the ancients as being disruptive. Indeed, the very concept of chaos was still considered equivalent to strife and treated as a negative. "No wonder things are all screwed up," they concluded, "they have got it all backwards." They found that the principle of disorder was every much as significant as the principle of order.

With this in mind, they studied the strange yin-yang. During a meditation one afternoon, a voice came to them:

This is **THE SACRED CHAO**. I appoint you keepers of It. Therein you will find anything you like. **Speak of Me as DISCORD**, to show contrast to the pentagon. Tell constricted mankind that there are no rules, unless they choose to invent rules. Keep close the words of Syadasti: **'TIS AN ILL WIND THAT BLOWS NO MINDS.**

And remember that there is no tyranny in the State of Confusion. For further information, consult your pineal gland.

"What is this?" mumbled one to the other. "A religion based on The Goddess of Confusion? It is utter madness!"

And with those words, each looked at the other in absolute awe. Omar began to giggle. Mal began to laugh. Omar began jumping up and down. Mal was hooting and hollering to beat all hell. And amid squeals of mirth and with tears on their cheeks, each appointed the other to be high priest of his own madness, and together they declared themselves to be a society of Discordia, for what ever that may turn out to be.

NEW STORY OF CHAOS

024

DIRUIT AEDIFICAT MUTAT QUADRATA ROTUNDUS
—**Horace**

Kerry Thornley

025

DO NOT REJECT THESE TEACHINGS AS FALSE BECAUSE I AM CRAZY. THE REASON THAT I AM CRAZY IS BECAUSE THEY ARE TRUE.

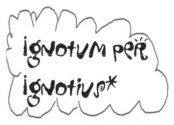

ignotum per ignotius*

The meaning of this is unknown

A ZEN STORY

by Camden Benares
The Court of Five Headmaster
Camp Meeker Cabal

A serious young man found the conflicts of early-21st Century America confusing. He went to many people seeking a way of resolving within himself the discords that troubled him, but he remained troubled.

One night in a coffee house, a self-ordained Zen Master said to him, "Go to the dilapidated mansion you will find at this address which I have written down for you. Do not speak to those who live there; you must remain silent until the moon rises tomorrow night. Go to the large room on the right of the main hallway, sit in the lotus position on top of the rubb in the northeast corner, face the corner, and meditate."

026

He did as the Zen Master instructed. His meditation was frequently interrupted by worries. He worried whether or not the rest of the plumbing fixtures would fall from the second floor bathroom to join the pipes and other trash he was sitting He worried how would he know when the moon rose on the next night. He worried about what the people walked through the room said about him.

His worrying and meditation were disturbed when, as if in a test of his faith, ordure fell from the second floor onto him. At that time two people walked into the room. The first asked the second who the man sitting thre was. The second replied "Some say he is a holy man. Others say he is a shit-head."

Hearing this, the man was enlightened.

027

WHAT WE KNOW
ABOUT ERIS (not much)

The Romans left a likeness of Her for posterity. She was shown as a grotesque woman with a pale and ghastly look, Her eyes afire, Her garment ripped and torn, and was concealing a dagger in Her Boson. Actually, most women look pale and ghastly when concealing a chilly dagger their bosoms.

028

No girdle ever cured a pregnacy.

029

Her geneology is from the Greeks and it is uttlerly confused. Either She was the twin of Aries and the daughter of Zeus and Hera; or She was the daughter Nyx, goddess of night (who was either the daugher or wife of Chaos, or both), and Nyx's brother, Erebus, and whose brothers and sisters include Death, Doom, Mockery, Misery, and Friendship. She begat Forgetfullness, Quarrels, Lies, and a bunch of gods and goddessess like that.

One day Mal-2 consulted his Pineal Gland* and asked Eris if She really created all of those terrible things. She told him that She had always liked the Old Greeks, but that they cannot be trusted with historic matters. "They were," She added, "victims of indigestion, you know."

Suffice it to say that Eris is not hateful or malicious. But She is mischievous—and does get a little bitchy at time.

030

THE PINEAL GLAND is where each and every one of us can talk to Eris. If you have trouble activating your Pineal, then try the appendix which does almost as well. References: DOGMA I, METAPHYSICS #3, "The Indoctrine of The Pineal Gland."

THE BATTLE HYMN
OF THE ERISTOCRACY

by Lord Omar

VERSE

Mine brain has meditated on the spinning of the Chaos; It is
hovering o'er the table where the Chiefs of Staff are now
Gathered in discussion of the dropping of the Bomb;
Her Apple Corps is strong;

CHORUS

Grand (and gory) Old Discordja!
Grand (and gory) Old Discordia!
Grand (and gory) Old Discordja!
Her Apple Corps is strong!

VERSE

She was not invited to the party that they held on Limbo Peak;*
So She threw a Golden Apple, 'sted of turn'n t'other cheek!
O it cracked the Holy Punchbowl and it made the nectar leak;
Her Apple Corps is strong!

* "Limbo Peak" refers to Old Limbo Peak, commonly called by the Greeks "Ol' Limb' Peak."

031

Discordian Eristocracy

What would a major world religion be without a ponderous hierarchy of pretentious titles to confuse, awe and madden the people with? Reasonable, that's what. We won't stand for that kind of non-nonsense around here.

The Church of Pentaversal Discord—a phrase just coined, but applied retroactively so that it predates time—has put together a suitably ridiculous Chutes and Ladders-type hierarchy of Who May Do What to Whom. *(There are those who would suggest that this has already been done adequately in the POEE Disorganizational Matrix, but as a member of a progressive belaboring union, I am unlawfully bound to suggest that such people get outta my face before I call for a walk-all-over and a picketting [which, in this context, very much resembles a staking— vampire-style]).*

At the bottom in this house of cards are, of course, the Popes. It should be noted that every man, woman, child and platypus, living, dead or otherwise, is an honest-to-Goddess Pope of Discordia, and thus infallible. Go get your Pope Card. **033**

*WRITTEN, IN SOME SENSE, BY MAL-2

You may think that this causes all sorts of trouble when Popes disagree—and you'd be right; you're a Pope, after all, but you'd be wrong because I'm a Pope too, you see.

Actually, when Popes disagree, it's a Wonderful Thing®, because thereby is the Divine Humour of Eris brought to full fruition. By believing every sort of contradictory thing—individually and as a group—Popes make these things True and Manifest as opposed to True and Unmanifest, and thus bear forth the Great Joke.

Consider this quote from the Holy Scripture, the *Principia Discordia*:

Malaclypse the Younger: *Everything is true.*
Greater Pope: *Even false things?*
Mal2: *Even false things are true.*
Greater Pope: *How can that be?*
Mal2: *I don't know, man, I didn't do it.*

Next up on the totem pole are the POEE (Paratheo-anametamystikhood Of Eris Esoteric [pronounced ``poee''] Chaplins, who have been ordained by reading Sacred Text (like this, for instance. Congratulations). Still higher than them are the POEE Priests, ordained by Mal^2 himself.

The pinnacles ("for pointy like unto a picket fence is the structure of the Church of Pentaversal Discord") of Discordianism are the Episkopossum—whose titles are, after all, capitalized. They are the ones whose visions of Eris transcend what IS, forcing them to create something which IS Not but Will Be If You Just Relax and Wait for a Second (jeez, you're pushy).

They create their own Cabals from the Hebrew "Kaballah," or "collection of absurdities for the unenlightened to take seriously'," often with nifty names.

Of course, since you're a Pope, you can decide that you, personally, are at the head of the Pentaversal Church and that Chaplins are much more enlightened than Priests (since they've gone to all the trouble of reading Sacred Text and ordaining themselves, while Priests were ordained by someone else), and therefore all of this is a steaming heap of dung (even though it's True), and you'd be right— but mistaken.

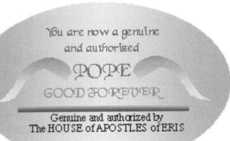

You are now a genuine and authorized

POPE

GOOD FOREVER

Genuine and authorized by
The HOUSE of APOSTLES of ERIS

035

036

You have a lopsided pineal gland!

Well, probably you do have one, and it's unfortunate because lopsided Pineal Glands have perverted the Free Spirit of Man, and subverted Life into a frustrating, unhappy and hopeless mess.

Becoming a Discordian will help you to:

➤ Balance your Pineal Gland and reach spiritual Illumination.

➤ Discover your salvation through ERIS, THE GODDESS OF CONFUSION.

➤ Turn your miserable mess into a beautiful, joyful, and splendid mess.

So read on!

PINEAL GLAND

A small, reddish gray, vascular, conical body of rudimentary glandular structure found in the brain and having no known function.

PINEAL GLAND

Well, having no known function for the Normals, anyway.

It is the psycho-metaphysical link between Eris and Her children, the point where the Realm of Ideas (and silly ones at that) touches the World of Substance, the elusive bridge known to the Norse as Bifrost, the long-sought-after fulcrum around which the quantum vectors of chance turn like a carousel - the Large Intestine, if you will, connecting the Discordian Insanity to that which it shovels.

—Funk & Wagnall's (Cheezy) Desk Dictionary:

037

KING KONG
DIED FOR
YOUR SINS

038

JOSHUA NORTON CABAL

Surrealists, Harlequinists, Absurdists,
and Zonked Artists Melee

POEE
is one manifestation of
THE DISCORDIAN SOCIETY
about which
you will learn more
and understand
less.   039

We
are a tribe
of philosophers, theologians,
magicians, clowns,
and similar maniacs
who are intrigued
with
ERIS
GODDESS OF CONFUSION
and with
Her
Doings.

INSPECTED
FOR WHOLESOMENESS
BY
★ U.S. ★
DEPARTMENT OF
AGRICULTURE
P-00

Official
DISCORDIAN SOCIETY
Hail Eris

Test Question:

If they are our brothers,
how come we can't eat them?

from Topanga Cabal—
THE TWELVE FAMOUS BUDDHA MINDS SCHOOL:

040

Abbey of the Barbarous Relic

The Five Commandments
The PENTABARF

THERE IS NO GODDESS BUT **ERIS**

The PENTABARF was discovered by the hermit Apostle Zarathud in the Fifth Year of the Caterpillar. He found them carved in gilded stone, while building a sun deck for his cave, but their import was lost for they were written in a mysterious cypher.

However, after 10 weeks and 11 hours of intensive scrutiny he discerned that the message could be read by standing on his head and viewing it upside down.

041

DISCORDIANS FLY BY NIGHT

KNOW YE THIS 0 MAN OF FAITH!

I. There is no Goddess but Goddess and She is Your Goddess. There is no Erisian Movement but The Erisian Movement and it is The Erisian Movement. And every Golden Apple Corps is the beloved home of a Golden Worm.

II. A Discordian Shall Always use the Official Discordian Document Numbering System.

III. A Discordian is Required during his early Illumination to Go Off Alone & Partake Joyously of a Hot Dog on a Friday. This Devotive Ceremony to Remonstrate against the popular Paganisms of the Day: of Catholic Christendom—no meat on Friday, of Judaism—no meat of Pork, of Hindic Peoples—no meat of Beef, of Buddhists—no meat of animal, and of Diacordians—no Hot Dog Buns.

IV. A Discordian shall Partake of No Hot Dog Buns, for such was the Solace of Our Goddess when She was Confronted with The Original Snub.

V. A Discordian is Prohibited from Believing What he Reads.

IT IS SO WRITTEN! SO BE IT.
HAIL DISCORDIA!

PROSECUTORS WILL BE TRANSGRESSICUTED.

043

"Did you know that there is a million bucks hidden in the house next door?" "But there is no house next door." "No? Then let's go build one!"

—MARX

WOW!

044

FNORDS ⇒ FNORD, FNORD, FNORD, FNORD, FNORD, FNORD, FNORD, FNORD, FNORD, FNORD,

****
Momomoto, Famous Japanese, can swallow his nose
****

I CANNOT ESCAPE THEM
NO MATTER HOW I TRY
THEY WAIT FOR ME EVERYWHERE
I CANNOT PASS THEM BY.

DRIVING DOWN THE STREET
I SEE "JESUS IS LORD"
AND THEN IMMEDIATELY AFTER
I HEAR THE WORD "FNORD!"

INNOCUOUS SAYINGS AND PARABLES
AND ON THE EVENING NEWS
I HEAR THE WORD "FNORD!"
AND SUDDENLY I'M CONFUSED

I SIT ALONE IN MY ROOM
AND I'M FEELING RATHER BORED
I TURN ON THE TUBE AND GUESS WHAT?
I HEAR THE WORD "FNORD!"

ON PRAYER

al 2 was once asked by one of his
Disciples if he often prayed to Eris.
He replied with these words:

*No, we Erisians seldom pray, it is
much too dangerous. Charles
Fort has listed many factual
incidences of ignorant people
confronted with, say, a drought,
and then praying fervently and
then getting the entire village
wiped out in a torrential flood.*

046

Heaven is down.
Hell is up.
This is proven by the fact
that the planets and stars
are orderly in their
movements,
while down on earth
we come close to the
primal chaos.
There are four other
proofs, but I forget them.

—**Josh the Drill**
KING KONG KABAL

047

Remember:

King Kong

Died For

Your Sins

DISSOCIATION OF IDEAS

"Surrealism aims at the total transformation of the mind and all that resembles it." —**Breton**

THE INSIDE STORY!

THE **LAW** OF FIVES

The Law of Fives is one of the oldest Erisian Mysterees. It was first revealed to Good Lord Omar and is one of the great contributions to come from The Hidden Temple of The Happy Jesus.

POEE subscribes to the Law of Fives of Omar's sect. And POEE also recognizes the Holy 23 (2+3=5) that is incorporated by Episkopos Dr. Mordecai Malignatius, KNS into his Discordian sect, The Ancient Illuminated Seers of Bavaria.

049

The Law of Fives states simply that:

All things happen in fives, or are divisible by or are multiples of five or are somehow directly or indirectly appropriate to 5.

The Law of Fives is never wrong.

In the Erisian Archives is an old memo from Omar to Mal 2: "I find the Law of Fives to be more and more manifest the harder I look."

MORE!

In Greek mythology, **Chaos** or **Khaos** is the primeval state of existence from which the first gods appeared.

In <u>Greek</u> it is É¥ÉøÉÕV, which is usually pronounced similarly to "house", but correctly in ancient Greek as "kh-a-oss"; it means "gaping void", from the verb É'Éø<<ÉÀÉ>> "gape, be wide open", Indo-European *"ghen-," *"ghn-"; compare English "chasm" and "yawn", Anglo-Saxon *geanian* = "to gape".

THE MYTH OF THE APPLE OF DISCORD

It seems that Zeus was preparing a wedding banquet for Peleus and Thetis and did not want to invite Eris because of Her reputation as a trouble maker.

This made Eris angry, and so She fashioned an apple of pure gold and inscribed upon it *KALLISTI—To The Prettiest One*—and on the day of the fete She rolled it into the banquet hall and then left to be alone and joyously partake of a hot dog.

Eris left an apple for "The Prettiest One".

Now, three of the invited goddesses, Athena, Hera, and Aphrodite, each immediately claimed it to belong to herself because of the inscription. And they started fighting, and they started throwing punchs all over the place and everything.

Finally Zeus calmed things down and declared that an arbitrator must be selected, which was a reasonable suggestion, and all agreed. He sent them to a shepherd of Troy, whose name was Paris because his mother had had a lot of gaul and had married a Frenchman; but each of the sneaky goddesses tried to outwit the others by going early and offering a bribe to Paris.

Athena offered him Heroic War Victories, Hera offered him Great Wealth, and Aphrodite offered him The Most Beautiful Woman on Earth. Being a healthy young Trojan lad, Paris promptly accepted Aphrodite's bribe, so she got the apple and he got screwed.

As she had promised, she maneuvered earthly happenings so that Paris could have Helen—*the* Helen—then living with her husband Menelaus, King of Sparta. Anyway, everyone knows that the Trojan War followed when Sparta demanded their Queen back and that the Trojan War is said to be The First War among men.

Aphrodite with the Golden Apple.

And so we suffer because of The Original Snub. And so a Discordian is to partake of No Hot Dog Buns

Do you believe that?

052

*This is called THE DOCTRTNE OF THE ORIGINAL SNUB.
**There is historic disagreement concerning whether this apple was of metalic gold or acapulco.
***Actually there were five goddesses, but the Greeks did not know of the Law of Fives.*

No
apple
for
Athena!

053

Aphrodite

APHRODITE FLEW OFF WITH HER GOLD APPLE
BECAUSE SHE WAS THE PRETTIEST ONE!

HOLY NAMES

Discordians have a tradition of assuming **HOLY NAMES**.
This is not unique with Erisianism, of course.
I suppose that Pope Paul is the son of Mr.& Mrs. VI?

There are also TITLES OF **MYSTICAL** IMPORT.

054

ZEUS

THE ORIGINAL SNUB: ZEUS DIDN'T INVITE ERIS TO THE
WEDDING BECAUSE SHE IS A TROUBLE MAKER. SO ERIS
FASHIONED A GOLDEN APPLE JUST TO MAKE TROUBLE.

AN ERISIAN HYMN

by Rev. Dr. Mungojerry Grindlebone, KOB
Episkopoe, THE RAVILLE APPLE PANTHERS

Onward Christian Soldiers,
Onward Buddhist Priests.
Onward, Fruits of Islam,
Fight till youre deceased.
Fight your little battles,
Join in thickest fray;
For the Greater Glory,
of Dis-cord-i-a.
Yah, yah,
yah,
Yah,
yah,
yah, yah.
Blffffffffffft!

Mr. Momomoto, famous Japanese WHO can SWALLOW his nose -has been exposed! It was recently that it was Mr. Momomoto's brother WHO has been doing ALL OF THIS Nose swallowing

055

056

OLD POEE SLOGAN:

When is doubt, fuck it. When not in doubt ... get in doubt!

Do Not Bend

DO
NOT
PULL
ON
YELLOW
TIP

καλλχτ

PLEASE DO NOT USE THIS
DOCUMENT AS TOILET TISSUE. *

*THIS AIN'T NO OUT-HOUSE, BUB!

057

BELIEVE IN NOTHING
BELIEFS ARE DANGEROUS.
BELIEFS ALLOW THE MIND
TO STOP FUNCTIONING.
A NON-FUNCTIONING MIND
IS CLINICALLY DEAD.

058

GENERAL LICENSE

GENERAL LICENSE was Sgt. Pepper's Commander

PERPETUAL DATE CONVERTER
FROM GREGORIAN TO POEE CALENDAR

						SM	BT	PD	PP	SO	
Jan	1	2	3	4	5	1	2	3	4	5	Chs
	6	7	8	9	10	6	7	8	9	10	
	11	12	13	14	15	11	12	13	14	15	
	16	17	18	19	20	16	17	18	19	20	
	21	22	23	24	25	21	22	23	24	25	
	26	27	28	29	30	26	27	28	29	30	
	31	1	2	3	4	31	32	33	34	35	
Feb	5	6	7	8	9	36	37	38	39	40	
	10	11	12	13	14	41	42	43	44	45	
	15	16	17	18	19	46	47	48	49	50	
	20	21	22	23	24	51	52	53	54	55	
	25	26	27	28*	1	56	57	58	59	60	
Mar	2	3	4	5	6	61	62	63	64	65	
	7	8	9	10	11	66	67	68	69	70	
	12	13	14	15	16	71	72	73	1	2	Dsc
	17	18	19	20	21	3	4	5	6	7	
	22	23	24	25	26	8	9	10	11	12	
	27	28	29	30	31	13	14	15	16	17	
Apr	1	2	3	4	5	18	19	20	21	22	
	6	7	8	9	10	23	24	25	26	27	
	11	12	13	14	15	28	29	30	31	32	
	16	17	18	19	20	33	34	35	36	37	
	21	22	23	24	25	38	39	40	41	42	
	26	27	28	29	30	43	44	45	46	47	
May	1	2	3	4	5	48	49	50	51	52	
	6	7	8	9	10	53	54	55	56	57	
	11	12	13	14	15	58	59	60	61	62	
	16	17	18	19	20	63	64	65	66	67	
	21	22	23	24	25	68	69	70	71	72	
	26	27	28	29	30	73	1	2	3	4	Cfn
	31	1	2	3	4	5	6	7	8	9	
Jun	5	6	7	8	9	10	11	12	13	14	
	10	11	12	13	14	15	16	17	18	19	
	15	16	17	18	19	20	21	22	23	24	
	20	21	22	23	24	25	26	27	28	29	
	25	26	27	28	29	30	31	32	33	34	
	30	1	2	3	4	35	36	37	38	39	

						SM	BT	PD	PP	SO	
Jul	5	6	7	8	9	40	41	42	43	44	Cfn
	10	11	12	13	14	45	46	47	48	49	
	15	16	17	18	19	50	51	52	53	54	
	20	21	22	23	24	55	56	57	58	59	
	25	26	27	28	29	60	61	62	63	64	
	30	31	1	2	3	65	66	67	68	69	
Aug	4	5	6	7	8	70	71	72	73	1	Bcy
	9	10	11	12	13	2	3	4	5	6	
	14	15	16	17	18	7	8	9	10	11	
	19	20	21	22	23	12	13	14	15	16	
	24	25	26	27	28	17	18	19	20	21	
	29	30	31	1	2	22	23	24	25	26	
Sep	3	4	5	6	7	27	28	29	30	31	
	8	9	10	11	12	32	33	34	35	36	
	13	14	15	16	17	37	38	39	40	41	
	18	19	20	21	22	42	43	44	45	46	
	23	24	25	26	27	47	48	49	50	51	
	28	29	30	1	2	52	53	54	55	56	
Oct	3	4	5	6	7	57	58	59	60	61	
	8	9	10	11	12	62	63	64	65	66	
	13	14	15	16	17	67	68	69	70	71	
	18	19	20	21	22	72	73	1	2	3	Afm
	23	24	25	26	27	4	5	6	7	8	
	28	29	30	31	1	9	10	11	12	13	
Nov	2	3	4	5	6	14	15	16	17	18	
	7	8	9	10	11	19	20	21	22	23	
	12	13	14	15	16	24	25	26	27	28	
	17	18	19	20	21	29	30	31	32	33	
	22	23	24	25	26	34	35	36	37	38	
	27	28	29	30	1	39	40	41	42	43	
Dec	2	3	4	5	6	44	45	46	47	48	
	7	8	9	10	11	49	50	51	52	53	
	12	13	14	15	16	54	55	56	57	58	
	17	18	19	20	21	59	60	61	62	63	
	22	23	24	25	26	64	65	66	67	68	
	27	28	29	30	31	69	70	71	72	73	

[1970 = 3136] [Next St. Tibs Day in 3138]

059

"THE FIVE LAWS HAVE ROOT IN AWARENESS."

Che Fung (Ezra Pound, Canto 85)

THE POEE MYSTREE OATH

The Initiate swears the following:
FLYING BABY SHIT!!!

Brothers of the Ancient Illuminated Seers
of Bavaria sect may which to substitute
the German:
FLIEGENDE KINDERSCHEISSE!

or perhaps
WIECZNY KWIAT WTADZA!!!!!

which is
EWIGE BLUMENKRAFT

in Polish.

060

Sacred Document of the Frogs
73 Days hath Chaos, Discord, Confusion,
Bureaucracy and Aftermath.

—Old Erisian poem

THERE ARE TRIVIAL
TRUTHS & THERE ARE
GREAT TRUTHS. THE
OPPOSITE OF A TRIVIAL
TRUTH IS PLAINLY
FALSE. THE OPPOSITE
OF A GREAT TRUTH IS
ALSO TRUE.

—Neils Bohr

061

News Flash:

The 9th Curcuit U.S. Court has just ruled that apples are not permitted in any school, government building or on any public property because, Eve's dalliances not withstanding, apples are a religious symbol. Hence forth teachers may only accept bananas and oranges from their pets.

POEE DISORGANIZATIONAL MATRIX

V) THE HOUSE OF APOSTLES OF ERIS
FOR THE ERISTOCRACY AND THE CABALABLIA
A. The Five Apostles of Eris
B. The Golden Apple Corps (KSC)
C. Episkoposes of The Discordian Society
D. POEE Cabal Priests
E. Saints, Erisian Avatars, and Like Personages

IV) THE HOUSE OF THE RISING PODGE
FOR THE DISCIPLES OF DISCORDIA*
A. Office Of MY High Reverence, The Polyfather
B. Council of POEE Priests
C. The LEGION OF DYNAMIC DISCORD
D. Eristic Avatars
E. Ameristic Avatars

*<u>NOTE</u>: A, B, and C are POEE PROPER; while D and E are POEE IMPROPER

III) THE HOUSE OF THE RISING HODGE
FOR THE BUREAUCRACY
A. The Bureau of Erisian Archives
B. The Bureau of The POEE Epistolary, and The Division of Dogmas
C. The Bureau of Symbols, Emblems, Certificates and Such
D. The Bureau of Eristic Affairs, and The Administry for The Unenlightened Eristic Horde
E. The Bureau of Ameristic Affairs, aand The Administry for The Orders of Discordia

II) THE HOUSE OF THE RISING COLLAPSE

FOR THE 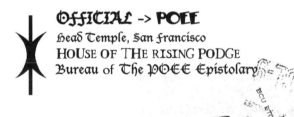AGEMENT OF LIBERATION OF ━━✖━━M, AND/OR THE
DISCOURAGEMENT OF THE IMMANENTIZING OF THE ESCHATON

A   The Breeze of Wisdom and/or The Wind of Insanity
B: The Breeze of Integrity and/or The Wind of Arrogance
C.   The Breeze of Beauty and/or The Wind of Outrages
D.   The Breeze of Love and/or The Wind of Bombast
E.   The Breeze of Laughter and/or The Wind of Bullshit

I) THE OUT HOUSE

FOR WHAT IS LEFT OVER

A.   Miscellaneous Avatars
B.   The Fifth Column
C.   **POEE** ->POPES<- everywhere
D.   Drawer "0" for OUT OF FILE
E.   Lost Documents and Forgotten Truths

OFFICIAL -> POEE
head Temple, San francisco
HOUSE OF THE RISING PODGE
Bureau of The POEE Epistolary

063

E
ECU ETO

SPORT

AN ICE CREAM PRODUCT

NIKE BY 90

PWS

CALIF

REGISTERED

OFFICE OF HIS HIGH REVERENCE
MALACLYPSE THE YOUNGER KSC
OPOVIG   HIGH PRIEST POEE

064

Whip this ass with What is Written
Grin like a ninny at What is Spoke.
Take refuge with thine wine in Nothing
behind Everything, as you hurry along
the Path.

THE PURPLE SAGE
HBT: The Book of Predications, Chap. 19

"In a way, we're a kind of Peace Corps."
—Maj A. Lincoln German, Training Director
Green Beret Special Warfare School, Ft. Bragg, N.C.

THE BEARER OF THIS CARD
IS A GENUINE AND AUTHORIZED

POPE

So please Treat Him Right
GOOD FOREVER

Genuine and authorized by The HOUSE of APOSTLES of ERIS

Every man, woman and child on this Earth is a genuine and authorized Pope.
Reproduce and distribute these cards freely•P.O.E.E. Head Temple, San Francisco

A=POPE= IS SOMEONE WHO IS NOT UNDER THE AUTHORITY OF THE AUTHORITIES *

THOU ART WHOLE

065

OK

The Numeral V Sign
Used by Old Roman Discordians, Illuminateus
Churchill, and innocent Hippies everywhere.

THE FIVE FINGERED HAND OF ERIS

The official symbol of **POEE** is here illustrated. It may be this, or any similar device to represent TWO OPPOSING ARROWS CONVERGING INTO A COMMON POINT. It may be vertical, horizontal, or else such, and it may be elaborated or simplified as desired.

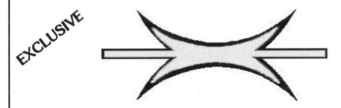

The esoteric name for this symbol is THE FIVE FINGERED HAND OF ERIS, commonly shortened to THE HAND.

NOTE: In the lore of western magic, the ⌒ is taken to symbolize horns, especially the horns of Satan or of diabolical beasties. The Five Fingered Hand of Eris, however, is not intended to be taken as satanic, for the "horns" are supported by another set of inverted "horns." Or maybe it is walrus tusks. I don't know what it is, to tell the truth.

067

POEE LEGIONNAIRE
DISCIPLES ARE
AUTHORIZED TO INITIATE
OTHERS AS DISCORDIAN
SOCIETY LEGIONNAIRES.

PRIESTS APPOINT THEIR
OWN DEACONS. THE
POLYFATHER ORDAINS
PRIESTS.

I DONO ABOUT THE
=POPES=.

068

"You will find that the STATE is the kind of ORGANIZATION which
though it does big things badly, it does small things badly too.
—John Kenneth Galbraith

POEE

POEE (pronounced "POEE") is an acronym for THE PARATHRO-ANAMETAMYSTIKHOOD OF ERIS ESOTERIC. The first part can be taken to mean "equivalent diety, reversing beyond mystique." We are not really esoteric, it's just that nobody pays much attention to us.

MY HIGH REVERENCE ALACLYPSE THE YOUNGER, AB, DD, KSC, is the High Priest of **POEE**, and **POEE** is grounded in his episkopotic revelations of the Goddess. He is called *The Omnibenevolent Polyfather of Virginity in Gold* .

069

The **POEE HEAD TEMPLE** is the Joshua Norton Cabal of The Discordian Society, which is located in Mal-2's pineal gland and can be found by temporaly and spacialy locating the rest of Mal-2.

POEE has no treasury, no by laws, no articles, no guides save Mal-2's pineal gland, and has only one scruple which Mal-2 keeps on his key chain.

POEE has not registered, incorporated, or otherwise chartered with the State, and so the State does not recognize **POEE** or **POEE** Ordinations, which is only fair, because **POEE** does not recognize the State.

NOTE: OUR MEMBERSHIP ROSTER IS OPEN TO PERSONS OF ALL RACES, NATIONAL ORIGINS AND HOBBIES..

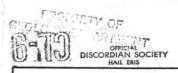

OFFICIAL
DISCORDIAN SOCIETY
HAIL ERIS

Application For Membership

In the Erisian Movement of the DISCORDIAN SOCIETY

1. Today's date   Yesterday's date

2. Purpose of this application: --membership in: a. Legion of Dynamic Discord   b. POEE   c. Bavarian Illuminati   d. All of the above   e. None of the above   f. Other--be *specific!*

3. Name   Holy Name

     Address

     If temporary, also give an address from which mail can be forwarded

4. Description: Born: [ ] yes [ ] no   Eyes: [ ] 2 [ ] other   Height: ....fl. oz.   Last time you had a haircut: Reason: Race: [ ] horse [ ] human   I. Q.: 150-200   200-250   250-300   over 300

5. History: Education - highest grade completed 1 2 3 4 5 6 over 6th Professional: On another ream of paper list every job since 1937 from which you have been fired.   Medical: On a seperate sheet labeled "confidential," list all major psychotic episodes experienced within the last 24 hours

6. Sneaky questions to establish personality traits I would rather a. live in an outhouse b. play in a rock group c. eat caterpillers. I wear obscene tattoos because . . . . . I have ceased raping little children [ ] yes [ ] no -- reason . . .

7. SELF-PORTRAIT

Answer
by wire.
SENDER WAITING!

Rev. Mungo
For Office Use Only-   acc. rej. burned

LICK HERE!

●

(You may be one of the lucky 25)

"THIS BOOK IS A MIRROR. WHEN A MONKEY LOOKS IN, NO APOSTLE LOOKS OUT." - LICHTENBERG

POEE has 5 DEGREES:

There is the neophyte,
  or **LEGIONNAIRE DISCIPLE**.

The **LEGIONNAIRE DEACON**,
  which is catching on.

An Ordained **POEE PRIEST/PRIESTESS**
  or a **CHAPLIN**.

The **HIGH PRIEST**,
  the Polyfather.

And **POEE**
 **POEE**

◻71

POEE & IT'S PRIESTS

IF YOU LIKE ERISIANISM AS IT IS PRESENTED ACCORDING TO MAL-2, THEN YOU MAY WISH TO FORM YOUR OWN POEE CABAL AS A POEE PRIEST AND YOU CAN GO DO A BUNCH OF POEE PRIESTLY THINGS. A "POEE CABAL" IS EXACTLY WHAT YOU THINK IT IS.

THE HIGH PRIEST MAKES NO DE- MANDS ON HIS PRIESTS, THOUGH HE DOES RATHER EXPECT GOOD WILL OF THEM. THE OFFICE OF THE POLYFATHER IS TO POINT, NOT TO TEACH. ONCE IN A WHILE, HE EVEN LISTENS.

072

SHOULD YOU FIND THAT YOUR OWN
REVELATIONS OF THE GODDESS BECOME
SUBSTANTIALLY DIFFERENT TFROM THE
REVELATIONS OF MAL-2, THEN PERHAPS THE
GODDESS HAS PLANS FOR YOU AS AN
EPIAKOPOS, AND YOU MIGHT CONSIDER
CREATING YOUR OWN SECT FROM SCRATCH,
UNHINDERED. EPISKOPOSES ARE NOT COMPETING
WITH EACH OTHER, AND THEY ARE ALL POEE
PRIESTS ANYWAY (AS SOON AS I LOCATE THEM).
THE POINT IS THAT
EPISKOPOSES ARE
DEVELOPING SEPARATE
PATHS TO THE ERISIAN
MOUNTAIN TOP.

SEE THE SECTION "DISCORDIAN SOCIETY."

074

HIP-2-3-4, HIP-2-3-4

Go to your Left-Right . . .

The Honest
Book of Truth

075

And through Omar did bid the
Collector of Garbage, in words that
were both sweet and bitter, to
surrender back the cigar box
containing the cards designated by the
Angel as The Honest Book of Truth, the
Collector was to him as one who might
be smitten deaf, saying only: "Gainst
the rules, y'know."

HBT: The Book of EXplanations, Chap. 2

The Honest Book of Truth being a BIBLE of the Erisian Movement and How It was
Revealed to Episkopos LORD OMAR KHYYAM RAVENHURST, KSC; Bull Goose of
Limbo; and Master Pastor of the Church Invisible of The Laughing Chris, Hidden
Temple of the Happy Jesus, Laughng Buddha Jesus (LBJ) Ranch.

ORDINATION
AS A POEE PRIEST

THERE ARE NO PARTICULAR QUALIFICATIONS FOR
ORDINATION BECAUSE IF YOU WANT TO BE A POEE
PRIEST THEN YOU MUST UNDOUBTEDLY QUALIFY.
WHO COULD POSSIBLY KNOW BETTER THAN YOU
WHETHER OR NOT YOU SHOULD BE ORDAINED?

AN ORDAINED POEE PRIEST OR PRIESTESS IS
DEFINED AS "ONE WHO HOLDS AN ORDINATION
CERTIFICATE FROM THE OFFICE OF THE
POLYFATHER."

RETURN TO
RESTRICTED ROOM
Do not pass "Go". Do not collect $200.

076

NOTE TO POEE PRIESTS:

THE POLYFATHER WISHES TO REMIND ALL ERISIANS THE POEE WAS CONCEIVED NOT AS A COMMERCIAL ENTER-PRISE AND THAT YOU ARE REQUESTED TO KEEP YOUR COOL WHEN SEEKING FUNDS FOR POEE CABALS OR WHEN SPREAD-ING THE POEE WORD VIA THE MAR-KET PLACE.

I am the PolyFather and I am coming to get you. So you better brush your teeth.

077

THE ERISIAN AFFIRMATION

BEFORE THE GODDESS ERIS,
I (name or holy name) , do herewith declare myself a **POEE BROTHER OF THE LEGION OF DYNAMIC DISCORD**.

HAIL HAIL HAIL HAIL HAIL
ERIS ERIS ERIS ERIS ERIS
ALL HAIL DISCORDIA.,

The presiding POEE Official (if any) responds:

ALL HAIL
DISCORDIA!

The presiding POEE Official (if any) responds:

ALL HAIL DISCORDIA!

THIS IS St. GULIK. HE IS THE MESSENGER OF THE GODDESS. A DIFFERENT AGE FROM OURS CALLED HIM HERMAS. MANY PEOPLE CALLED HIM BY MANY NAMES. HE IS A Roach.

Sometimes humor is serious. Sometimes seriousness is humorous. Either way it is irrelevant.

079

Tao Fa Tsu-Dan

THE hidden STONE RiPENS FAST,

THEN LAiD BARE LIKE A TURNIP

CAN EASiLY BE CUT OUT AT LAST

BUT EVEN THEN THE DANGER ISN'T PAST.

THAT MAN LiVES bEST WHO'S FAIN

TO LiVE HALF MAD, HALF SANE.

—FLEMiSH PoET JAN VAN

STiJEVOORT, 1524.

DONT PHONE

Find the Goddess Eris
within your pineal gland

POEE

080

Seek into the Chao if
thou wouldst be wise
And find ye delight in
Her Great Surprise!
Look into the Chao if
thou wantest to
know What's in
a Chao and
why it ain't
so!

HBT: The Book of Advice

Common sense tells you that the world is flat.

082　Hon. Emperor Norton

One night a gang of vigilantes gathered for a raid on San Francisco's Chinatown. All that stood in their way was the solitary figure of Norton.

A sane man would not have been there in the first place. A rational man would have tried reasoning. A moralist would have scolded them.

On lookers expected Norton to loudly order the thugs to cease and desist in the name of His Royal Imperial authority. All such tacks would probably have been futile, and Norton resorted to none of these futile tactics.

Instead, Norton simply bowed His head in silent prayer. The vigilantes dispersed.

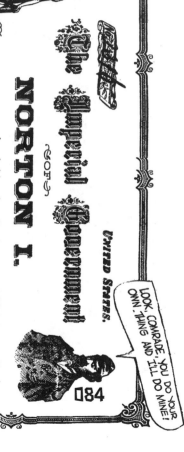

THE IMPERIAL GOVERNMENT OF NORTON I.

UNITED STATES.

The Imperial Government

~OF~

NORTON I.

Promises to pay the holder hereof the sum of *Fifty Cents* in the year 1880, with interest at 7 per cent. per annum from date; the principal and interest to be convertible, at the option of the holder, at maturity, into 20 years 7 per cent. Bonds or payable in Gold Coin.

Given under our Royal hand and seal this ___19___ day of _August_ 187_9_

Norton I.
Emperor ~

CUDDY & HUGHES, Printers to His Majesty Norton I, 611 Sansome Street, S. F.

084

Security Last Intergalactic
Bank of Malaclypse
ENDORCED AND GUARANTEED

IN GODDESS WE TRUST

LOOK, COMRADE, YOU DO YOUR OWN THING AND I'LL DO MINE!

Live like Norton!

Write your local politician and demand a Constitutional Amendment giving all people the right to live as Emperor Joshua A. Norton did.

MORD says that Omar says that we are all unicorns anyway..

DOES ZOOLOGY INCLUDE HUMANS?

HAIL ERIS !

086

HOW TO START A POEE CABAL
WITHOUT MESSING AROUND WITH THE POLYFATHER

If you cannot find the Polyfather, or having found him, don't want anything to do with him, you are still authorized to form your own POEE CABAL and do Priestly Things, using the *Principia Discordia* as a guide. Your Offical Rank will be POEE CHAPLIN for The Legion of DYNAMIC DISCORD, which is exactly the same as POEE PRIEST except that you don't have an Ordination Certificate.

You are a Goddess.
Live like one!

HOW TO BECOME
A POEE CHAPLIN

1. Write the *The Erisian Affirmation* in five copies.

2. Sign and nose print each copy.

3. Send one to

    The President of the United States.

4. Send one to:
    The California State Bureau of Furniture and Bedding, 1021 IDI Street, Sacramento CA 94814

5. Nail one to a telephone pole. Hide one. And burn the other.

    Then consult your pineal gland.

088

The words you are now reading
are your ordination.

HAIL ERIS !

TRIP 5

THE POEE BAPTISMAL RITE

This Mysteree Rite is not required for initiation, but it is offered by many POEE Priests to proselytes who desire a formal ceremony.

1. The Priest and four Brothers are arranged in a pentagon with the Initiate in the center facing the Priest. If possible the Brothers on the immediate right and left of the Priest should be Deacons. The Initiate must be totally naked to demonstrate that he is truly a human beingand not something else in disguise like a cabbage or something.

2. All persons in the audience and the pentagon-excepting the Priest-assume a squatting position and return to a standing position. This is repeated fout more times. This dance is symbolic of the humility of we Erisians.

κολλιχτι

3. The Priest begins:

I, (complete ~~Holy~~ Name-with Mystical Titles-and degrees-designations-~~offices,etc.~~), ORDAINED PRIEST OF THE PARATHEO- ANAMETAMYETIKHOOD OF ERIS ESOTERIC, WITH THE AUTHORITY INVESTED AT ME BY THE HIGH PRIEST OF IT, OFFICE OF THE POLYFATHER, THE HOUSE OF THE RISING PODGE, POEE HEAD TEMPLE; DO HEREWITH REQUIRE OF YE:

a) ARE YE A HUMAN BEING AND NOT A CABBAGE OR SOMETHING? The Initiate answers: YES.

b) THAT'S TOO BAD. DO YE WISH TO BETTER THYSELF? The Initiate answers: YES.

c) HOW STUPID. ARE YE WILLING TO BECOME PHILOSOPHICALLY ILLUMINIZED? He answers: YES.

d) VERY FUNNY. WILL YE DEDICATE YESELF TO THE HOLEY ERISIAN MOVEMENT? The Initiate answers: PROBABLY.

e) THEN SWEAR YE THE FOLLOWING AFTER ME: (The Priest here leads the Initiate in a recital of *The Erisian Affirmation.*) The Priest continues: THEN I DO HERE PROCLAIM YE POEE DISCIPLINE (name), LEGIONNAIRE OF THE LEGION OF DYNAMIC DISCORD. HAIL ERIS! HAIL HAIL! HAIL! YES!

4. All present rejoice grandly. The new Brother opens a large jug of wine and offers it to all who are present.

5. The Ceremony generally degenerates.

091

THE RECENT EXPOSE
THAT MR. MOMOMOTO, FAMOUS JAPANESE
WHO CAN SWALLOW HIS NOSE, CANNOT
SWALLOW HIS NOSE BUT HIS BROTHER CAN
HAS BEEN EXPOSED! IT IS MOMOMOTO
WHO CAN SWALLOW HIS NOSE. HE
SWALLOWED HIS BROTHER IN THE
SUMMER OF '44.

CORRECTION TO LAST
WEEK'S COPY: JOHNNY
SAMPLE IS OFFENSIVE
CORNERBACK FOR THE
NEW YORK JETS, NOT
FULLBACK AS STATED.
BOBBY TOLAN'S NAME IS NOT
RANDY, BUT MUD. ALL POWER TO THE
PEOPLE, AND BAN THE BOMB.

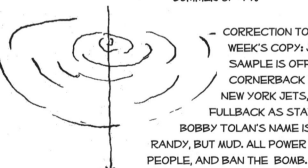

Hey, hook, line and sinker!

092

World Council of Churches Boutique

THE DISCORDIAN SOCIETY

The Discordian Society has no definition.

I sometimes think of it as a disorganization of Eris Freaks. It has been called a guerrilla mind theatre. Episkopos Randomfactor, Director of Purges of Our People's Underworld Movement sect in Larchmont, prefers "The World's Greatest Association of What-ever-it-is-that-we-are." Lady Mal thinks of it as a Renaissance Think Tank. Fang the Unwashed, WKC, won't say. You can think of it any way you like.

AN EPISKOPOS OF THE DISCORDIAN SOCIETY is one who prefers total autonomy, and creates his own Discordian sect as The Goddess directs him. He speaks for himself and for those that say that they like what he says.

THE LEGION OF DYNAMIC DISCORD:
A Discordian Society Legionnaire is one who prefers not to create his own sect.

093

If you want in on the Discordian Society
then declare yourself what you wish,
do what you like
and tell us about it
or
if you prefer
don't.

094

And the snake said, "Come on, Eve, take just a little bite."

5. Hung Mung slapped his buttocks, hopped about, and shook his head, saying, "I do not know! I do not know!"

—HBT: The Book of Gooks, Chap. 1

There are no rules anywhere.
The Goddess Prevails.

Some Episkoposes have
a one-man cabal.
Some work together.
Some never do explain.

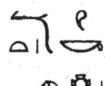
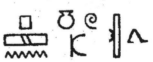

DULL BUT SINCERE FILLER

HAIL ERIS
ALL HAIL DISCORDIA
POEE

THE ANCIENT ILLUMINATED SEERS OF BAVARIA
Vigilance Lodge
Mad Malik, Hauptscheissmeister
Resident for Norton Cabal

D5
X

Discordian Society Super Secret Cryptographic Cypher Code

OF POSSIBLE INTEREST TO ALL DISCORDIANS, this information is herewith released from the vaults of A.I.S.B., under the auspices of Episkopos Dr. Mordecai Malignatius, KNS.

Sample Message: "Hail Eris"
Conversion:

A B C D E F G H I J K L M N O P Q R S T U V W X Y Z
1 2 3 4 5 6 7 8 9 10 11 12 13 14 15 16 17 18 19 20 21 22 23 24 25 26

Step 1. Write out message (HAIL ERIS) and put all vowels
   at end (HLRSAIEI)
Step 2. Reverse order (IEIASRLH)
Step 3. Convert to numbers (9-5-9-1-19-18-12-8)
Step 4. Put into numerical order (1-5-8-9-9-12-18-19)
Step 5. Convert back to letters (AEHIILRS)

This cryptographic cyper code is
GUARANTEED TO BE 100% UNBREAKABLE

097

OBEY THE SNAFU PRINCIPLE.

WHEN I GET TO THE BOTTOM
I GO BACK TO THE TOP OF
THE SLIDE WHERE I STOP
AND I TURN AND I GO FOR
A RIDE - THEN I GET TO THE
BOTTOM AND I SEE YOU
AGAIN! HELTER SKELTER!

John Lennon

Come here little boy and give
Eris a big Kiss.

098

Climb into the chao with a friend or two
And follow the Way it carries you,
Adrift like a Lunatic Lifeboat Crew
Over the Waves in whatever you do.

HBT: The Book of Advice, 1:3

099

THE GOLDEN APPLE CORPS

The Golden Apple Corps* is an honorary position for The Keepers of the Sacred Chao, so that they can put "KSC" after their names.

It says little,
does less,
means
nothing.

*Not to be confused with the Apple Corps Ltd.
of those four singers. We thought of it first.

ERIS CONTEMPATES FOR
3125 YEARS

SEASONS

1) Chaos — Patron Apostle Hung Mung
2) Discord — Patron Apostle Dr. Van Van Mojo
3) Confusion — Patron Apostle Sri Syadasti
4) Bureaucracy — Patron Apostle Zarathud
5) The Aftermath — Patron Apostle The Elder Malaclypse

DAYS OF THE WEEK

1) Sweetmorn
2) Boomtime
3) Pungenday
4) Prickle-Prickle
5) Setting Orange

*DAYS OF THE WEEK are named from the five Basic Elements:
Sweet
Boom
Pungent
Prickle
Orange

HOLYDAYS

A) **Apostle Holydays**
    1) Mungday
    2) Mojoday
    3) Syaday
    4) Zaraday
    5) Maladay
Each occurs on the 5th
day of the Season.

102

100c) **St. Tib's Day** - occurs once every 4 years (1+4=5) and is inserted between the 59th and 60th days of the Season of Chaos.

MILIARY

"Of course I'm crazy, but
that doesn't mean I'm wrong.
I'm mad, but not ill."
—Robert Anton Wilson
Werewolf Bridge

DO NOT CIRCULATE

The Eristan Movement does not discriminate against werewolves.

FOR YOUR
ENLIGHTENMENT **104**

THE PARABLE OF THE BITTER TEA

by Rev.Dr. Hypocratee Magoun, P.P.
POEE PRIEST, Okinawa Cabal

When Hypoc was through meditating with St.Gulik, he went there into the kitchen where he busied himself with preparing the feast and in his endeavor, he found that there was some old tea in a pan left standing from the night before, when he had in his weakness forgot about its making and had let it sit steeping for 24 hours. It was dark and murky and it was Hypoc's intention to use this old tea by diluting it with water. And again in his weakness, chose without further consideration and plunged into the physical labor of the preparations.

It was then when deeply immersed in the pleasure of that trip, he had a sudden loud clear voice in his head saying "it is bitter tea that involves you so." Hypoc heard the voice, but the struggle inside intensified, and the pattern, previously established with the physical laboring and the muscle messages coordinated and unified or perhaps coded, continued to exert their influence and Hypoc succummed to the pressure and he denied the voice.

And again he plunged into the physical orgy and completed the task, and Lo, as the voice had predicted, the tea was bitter.

FYI: The Greek geometrician **PYTHAGORAS** was not a typical aneristic personality.

He was what we call an **EXPLODED ANERISTIC** and an **AVATAR.**

We call him Archangel Pythagoras.

105

POEE is a bridge from PISCES to AQUARIUS

A Sermon on Ethics and Love

One day Mal-2 asked the messenger spirit Saint Gulik to approach the Goddess and request Her presence for some desperate advice. Shortly afterwards the radio came on by itself, and an ethereal female Voice said, **YES?**

"O! Eris! Blessed Mother of Man! Queen of Chaos! Daughter of Discord! Concubine of Confusion! O! Exquisite Lady, I beseech You to lift a heavy burden from my heart!"

What bothers you, Mal? You don't sound well.

"I am filled with fear and tormented with terrible visions of pain. Everywhere people are hurting one another, the planet is rampant with injustices, whole societies plunder groups of their own people, mothers imprison sons, children perish while brothers war. O, woe."

What is the matter with that, if it is what you want to do?

"But nobody wants it! Everybody hates it."

Oh, well, then stop.

At which moment She turned Herself into an aspirin commercial and left the Polyfather stranded alone with his species.

Polite children always remember that a church is the _____ of _____.

Will whoever stole Brother Reverend Magoun's porography please return it.

It is my firm belief that it is a mistake to hold firm beliefs.

CHAPTER 5: THE PIONEERS

= THE FIVE ApOSTLEs OF ERIS & WHO THEY BE =

1. HUNG MUNG
A Sage of Ancient China and Official Discordian Missionary to the Heathen Chinee. He who originally devised THE SACRED CHAO. Patron of The Season of Chaos. *Holyday: Jan 5.*

2. Dr. VAN VAN MOJO
A Head Doctor of Deep Africa and Maker of Fine Dolls D.H.V., Doctor of Hoodoo and Vexes, from The Greater Metropolitan Yorba Linda Jesus Will Save Your Bod Home Study Bible School; and F.I.H.G.W.P., *Fellow of the Intergalactic Haitian Guerrillas for World Peace.* Patron of The Season of Discord. *Holyday: Mar 19.*

108

NOTE: Erisians of the Laughing Chris sect are of the silly contention that Dr. Mojo is an imposter and that PATAMUNZO LINGANANDA is the True Second Apostle. Lord Omar claims that Dr.Mojo heaps hatred and curses upon Patonunzo, who sends only Love Vibrations in return. But we of the POEE sect know that Patamunzo is the Real Imposter, and that those vibrations of his are actually an attempt to subvert Dr. Mojols rightful apostilic authority by shaking him out of his wits.

3. SRI SYADASTI SYADAVAKTAVYA SYADASTI SYANNASTI SYADASTI CAVAKTAVYASCA SYADASTI SYANNASTI SYADAVATAVYASCA SYADASTI SYANNASTI SYADAVAKTAVYASCA (Commonly called just SRI SYADASTI)

His name is Sanskrit, and means: All affirmations are true in some sense, false in some sense, meaningless in some sense, true and false in some sense, true and meaningless in some sesne, false and meaingless in some sense, and true and flse and meaningless in some sense.

He is an Indian Pundit and Prince, born of the Peyotl Tribe, son of Gentle Chief Sun Flower Seed and the squaw Merry Jane. Patron to psychedelic type Discordians. Patron of The Season of Confusion. *Holyday: May 31.*

NOTE: Sri Syddasti should not be confused with BLESSED ST. GULIK THE STONED, who is not the same person but is the same Apostle.

4. ZARATHUD THE INCORRIGIBLE, sometimes called ZARATHUD THE STAUNCH.

A hard nosed Hermit of Medieval Europe and Chosphe Bible Banger. Dubbed "Offender of The Faith." Discovered the Five Commandments. Patron of The Season of Bureaucracy. *Holyday: Aug 12.*

109

5. THE ELDER MALACLYPSE.

A wandering Wiseman of Ancient Mediterrania ("MedTerra" or middle earth), who followed a 5-pointed Star through the alleys of Rome, Damascus, Baghdad, Jerusalem, Mecca and Cairo, bearing a sign that seemed to read "DOOM".(This is a misunderstanding. The sign actually read "DUMB". Mal-1 is a Non-Prophet.) Patron and namesake of Mal-2. Patron on The Season of The Aftermath. *Holyday: Oct 24.*

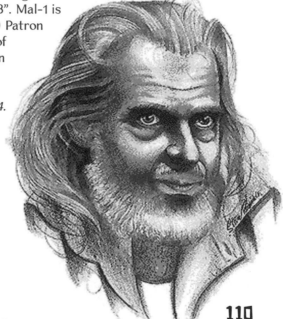

Sinister Dexter has a broken spirometer.

All statements are true in some sense, false in some sense, meaningless in some sense, true and false in some sense, true and meaningless in some sense, false and meaningless in some sense, and true and false and meaningless in some sense. A public service clarification by the Sri Syadasti School of Spiritual Wisdom, Wilmette.

The teachings of the Sri Syadasti School of Spiritual Wisdom are true in some sense, false in some sense, meaningless in some sense, true and false in some sense, true and meaningless in some sense, false and meaningless in some sense, and true and false and meaningless in some sense.

Patamunzo Lingananda
School of Higher Spiritual Wisdom, Skokie.
From *The Honest Book of Truth*

111

THE BOOK OF EXPLANATIONS
Chapter 1

1. There came one day to Lord Omar, Bull Goose of Limbo, a Messenger of Our Lady who told him of a Sacred Mound wherein was buried the Honest Book.

2. And the Angel of Eris bade of the Lord: Go ye hence and dig the Truth, that ye may come to know it and, knowing it, spread it and, spreading it, wallow in it and, wallowing in it, lie in it and, lying in the Truth, become a Poet of the Word and a Sayer of Sayings—an Inspiration to all men and Scribe to the Gods.

3. So Omar went forth to the Sacred Mound, which was to the East of Nullah, and thereupon he worked digging in the sand for five days and five nights but found no book.

4. At the end of five days and five nights of digging, it came to pass that Omar was exhausted. So he put his shovel to one side and bedded himself down on the sand, using as a pillow a Golden Chest he had uncovered on the first day of his labors.

5. Omar slept.

6. On the fifth day of his sleeping, Lord Omar fell into a Trance, and there came to him in the Trance a Dream, and there came to him in the Dream a Messenger of Our Lady who told him of a Sacred Grove wherein was hidden a Golden Chest.

7. And the Angel of Eris bade of the Lord: Go ye hence and lift the Stash, that ye may come to own it and, owning it, share it and,

112

sharing it, love in it and, loving in it, dwell in it and, dwelling in the Stash, become a Poet of the Word and a Sayer of Sayings—an Inspiration to all men and a Scribe to the Gods.

8. But Omar lamented, saying unto the Angel: What is this shit, man? What care I for the Word and Sayings? What care I for the Inspiration of all men? Wherein does it profit a man to be a Scribe to the Gods when the Scribes of the Govermnents do nothing, yet are paid better wages?

9. And, lo, the Angel waxed in anger and Omar was stricken to the Ground by an Invisible Hand and did not arise for five days and five nights.

10. And it came to pass that on the fifth night he drempt, and in his Dream he had a Vision, and in this Vision there came unto him a Messenger of Our Lady who entrusted to him a Rigoletto cigar box containing many filing cards, some of them in packs with rubber bands around, and upon these cards were sometimes written verses, while upon others nothing was written.

11. Thereupon the Angel Commanded the Lord: Take ye this *Honest Book of Truth* to thine bosom and cherish it. Carry it forth into The Land before Kings of Nations and Collectors of Garbage. Preach from it unto the RIghteous, that they may renounce their ways and repent.

113

suspended annihilation

CONVENTIONAL CHAOS

GREYFACE

I n the year 1166 B.C., a malcontented hunchbrain by the name of Greyface, got it into his head that the universe was as humorless as he, and he began to teach that play was sinful because it contradicted the ways of Serious Order. "Look at all the order about you," he said. And from that, he deluded honest men to believe that reality was a straightjacket affair and not the happy romance as men had known it.

It is not presently understood why men were so gullible at that particular time, for absolutely no one thought to observe all the *disorder* around them and conclude just the opposite. But anyway, Greyface and his followers took the game of playing at life more seriously than they took life itself and were known even to destroy other living beings whose ways of life differed from their own.

The unfortunate result of this is that mankind has since been suffering from a psychological and spiritual imbalance. Imbalance causes frustration, and frustration causes fear. And fear makes a bad trip.

Man has been on a bad trip for a long time now. It is called *THE CURSE OF GREYFACE.*

MANDALA

**NO TWO ELEMENTS INTERLOCK
BUT ALL FIVE DO INTERLOCK**

115

In times of medieval magic, the pentagon was the generic symbol for werewolves

Meanwhile, at the chinese laundromat . .

APOSTLE HUNG MUNG
comtemplates his navel.

The eminent 16th Century Mathemetician Cardan so detested Luther that he altered Luther's birthdate to give him an unfavorable horosope.

The Words of the Foolish and those of the Wise
Are not far apart in Discordian Eyes.

HBT: The Book of Advice, 2:2

COSMOLOGY*

The Book of Uterus
from *The Honest Book of Truth*
revealed to Lord Omar.

119

-I-

1. Before the beginning was the Nonexistent Chao, balanced in Oblivion by the Perfect Counterpush-pull of the Hodge and the Podge.

2. Whereupon, by an Act of Happenstance, the Hodge began gradually to overpower the Podge—and the Primal Chaos thereby came to be.

3. So in the beginning was the Primal Chaos, balanced on the Edge of Oblivion by the Perfect Counterpull-push of the Podge and the Hodge.

4. Whereupon, by the Law of Negative Reversal,* the Podge swiftly underpowered the Hodge and Everything broke loose.

5. And therein emerged the Active Force of Discord, the Subtle Manifestation of the Nonexistent Chao, to guide Everything along the Path back to Oblivion—that it might not become lost among Precepts of Order in the Region of Thud.

6. For asmuch as it was Active, the Force of Discord entered the State of Confusion, wherein it copulated with the Queen and begat ERIS, Our Lady of Discord and Gross Manifestation of the Nonexistent Chao.

7. And under Eris Confusion became established, and was hence called Bureaucracy; while over Bureaucracy Eris became established, and was hence called Discordia.

8. By the by it came to pass that the Establishment of Bureaucracy perished in a paper shortage.

9. Thus it was, in accord with the Law of Laws.

10. During and after the Fall of the Establishment of Bureaucracy was the Aftermath, an Age of Disorder in which calculation, computations, and reckonings were put away by the Children of Eris in Acceptance and Preparation for Return to Oblivion to be followed by a Repetition of the Universal Absurdity. Moreover of Itself the Coming of Aftermath waseth a Resurrection of the Freedom flowing Chaos.

HAIL ERIS!

11. Herein was set into motion the Eristic Pattern, which would Repeat Itself Five Times Over Seventy-three Times, after which nothing would happen. **120**

*WHICH IS NOT THE SAME AS DOGMA ! - METAPHYSICS #2, "COSMOLOGY" FROM BOOK OF UTERUS.

FIND PEACE WITH A CONTENTED CHAO.

121

"MU" is the Chinese ideogram for NO-THING

Cosomology Notes:

*COSMOLOGY should not be confused with DOGMA III—
"HISTORY CYCLES," which states that social progress
occurs in five cycles, the first three ("The Tricycle") of
which are THESIS, ANTITHESIS and PARENTHESIS; and the
last two ("The Bicycle") of which are CONSTERNATION
and MORAL WARPTITUDE.

**The LAW OF NEGATIVE REVERSAL states that if some-
thing does *not* happen then the exact opposite *will*
happen, only in exactly the opposite manner from that in
which it did not happen.

NOTE: It is from this text from *The Book of Uterus*, that POEE has based
its Erisian Calendar with the year divided into 5 Seasons of 73 days
each. Each of the Five Apostles of Eris has patronage over one Season.
A chart of the Seasons, Patrons, Days of the Week, Holydays, and a
perpetual Gregorian converter is included in this edition of *Discordia*.

The seeds of the **ORDERS OF DISCORDIA** were planted by Greyface into his early disciples. They form the skeleton of the Aneristic Movement, which over emphasizes the Principle of Order and is antagonistic to the necessary compliment, the Principle of Disorder. The Orders are composed of persons all hung up on authority, security and control; i.e., they are blinded by the Ameristic Illusion. They do not know that they belong to Orders of Discordia.

But we know.

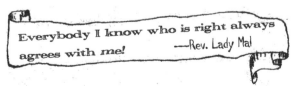

Everybody I know who is right always agrees with me!

—Rev. Lady Mal

The Five Orders of Discordia
("Them")
GEN. PANDAEMONIUM, COMMANDING

 124

1. The Military Order of **THE KNIGHTS OF THE FIVE SIDED TEMPLE.** THIS IS FOR ALL OF THE SOLDIERS AND UCRATS OF THE WORLD.

2. The Political Order of **THE PARTY FOR WAR ON EVIL.** THIS IS RESERVED FOR LAWMAKERS, CENSORS, AND THEIR ILK..

3. The Academic Order of **THE HEMLOCK FELLOWSHIP.** THEY COMMONLY INHABIT SCHOOLS AND UNIVERSITIES, AND DOMINATE MANY OF THEM.

4. The Social Order of **THE CITIZENS COMMITTEE FOR CON- CERNED CITIZENS.** THIS IS MOSTLY A GRASS ROOTS VERSION OF THE FORE PROFESSIONAL MILITARY, POLITICAL, ACADEMIC AND SACRED ORDERS.

5. The Sacred Order of **THE DEFAMATION LEAGUE.** NOT MUCH IS KNOWN ABOUT THE D.L., BUT THEY ARE VERY ANCIENT AND QUITE POSSIBLY WERE FOUNDED BY GREYFACE HIMSELF. IT IS KNOWN THAT THEY NOW HAVE ABSOLUTE DOMINATION OVER ALL ORGANIZED CHURCHES IN THE WORLD. IT IS ALSO BELIEVED THAT THEY HAVE BEEN COSTUMING CABBAGES AND PASSING THEM OFF AS HUMAN BEINGS.

A person belonging to one or more Order is just as likely to carry a flag of the counter-eatablishment as the flag of the establishment — just as long as it is a flag.

The following is quoted from Bergan Evans
on Norbert Weiner, Nuclear Physicist

The second concept Wiener has to establish is
that of entropy. Probability is a mathematical
concept· coming from statistics. Entropy comes from
physics. It is the assertion-established logically and
experimentally-that the universe· by its nature· is
"running down"· moving toward a state of inert
uniformity devoid of form· matter· hierarchy or
differentiation.

That is· in any given situation· less organiza-
tion· more chaos· is overwhelmingly more probable
than tighter organization or more order.

The tendency for entropy to increase in isolated
systems is expressed in the second law of
thermodayamics-perhaps the most pessimistic and
amoral formulation in all human thought.

It applies however· to a closed system-to something that is an isolated whole-not just a part.
Within such systems there may be parts· which draw
their energy from the whole· that are moving at
least temporarily· in the opposite direction· in them
order is increasing and chaos is diminishing.

Q. "How come a woodpecker doesn't bash its brains out?" A. Nobody has ever explained that.

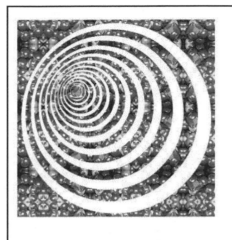

The whirlpools that swirl in a direction opposed to the main current are called "enclaves". And one of them is life - especially human life - which in a universe moving inexorably towards chaos moves toward increased order.

127

If the telephone rings today ... water it!

—Rev. Thomas, Gnostic N.Y.C. Cabal

ERIS

And, behold, thusly was the Law formulated: Imposition of Order = escalation of Disorder!

HBT: The Gospel According to Fred, 1:6.

"I SHOULD
HAVE BEEN A
PLUMBER."
—Albert
Einstein

"Grasshopper always wrong in argument with chicken"

Book of Chan
compiled by O.P.U. sect

= Zarathud's Enlightenment =

Before he became a hermit, Zarathud was a young Priest, and took great delight in making fools of his opponents in front of his followers.

One day Zarathud took his students to a pleasant pasture and there he confronted The Sacred Chao while She was contentedly grazing.

"Tell me, you dumb beast," demanded the Priest in his commanding voice, *"why don't you do something worthwhile. What is your Purpose in Life, anyway?"*

Munching the tasty grass, The Sacred Chao replied, *"MU"*.*

Upon hearing this, absolutely nobody was enlightened. Primarily because nobody could understand Chinese.

130

The Sacred Chao

The SACRED CHAO is the key to illumination. Devised by the Apostle Hung Mung in ancient China, it was modified and popularized by the Taoists and is sometimes called the YIN-YANG.

The Sacred Chao is not the Yin-Yang of the Taoists. It is the HODGE-PODGE of the Erisians. And, instead of a Podge spot on the Hodge side, it has a PENTA-GON which symbolizes the ANERISTIC PRINCIPLE, and instead of a Hodge spot on the Podge side, it depicts the GOLDEN APPLE OF DISCORDIA to symbolize the ERISTIC PRINCIPLE.

131

The Sacred Chao symbolizes absolutely everything anyone need ever know about absolutely anything, and more! It even symbolizes everything not worth knowing, depicted by the empty space surrounding the Hodge-Podge.

SOME PSYCHO METAPHYSICS.

If you are not hot for philosophy, best just skip it.

The Aneristic Principle is that of ***APPARENT ORDER***; the Eristic Principl is that of ***APPARENT DISORDER***. Both order and disorder are man made *concepts* and are artificial divisions of PURE CHAOS, which is a level deeper than is the level of distinction making.

With our concept making apparatus called "mind" we look at reality through the ideas-about-reality which our cultures give us. The ideas-about-reality are mistakenly labeled "reality" and unenlightened people are forever perplexed by the fact that other people, especially other cultures, see "reality" differently. It is only the ideas-about-reality which differ. Real (capital-T True) reality is a level deeper than is the level of concept.

We look at the world through windows on which have been drawn grids (concepts). Different philosophies use different grids. A culture is a group of people with rather similar grids. Through a window we view chaos, and relate it to the points on our grid, and thereby understand it. The ORDER is in the GRID. That is the ***Aneristic Principle***.

Western philosophy is traditionally concerned with contrasting one grid with another grid, and amending grids in hopes of finding a perfect one that will account for all reality and will, hence, (say—unenlightened westerners) be True. This is illusory; it is that we Erisians call the ***ANERISTIC ILLUSION***.

132

Some grids can be more useful than others, some more beautiful than others, some more pleasant than others, etc., but none can be more True than any other.

DISORDER is simply unrelated information viewed through some particular grid. But, like "relation", no-relation is a concept. Male, like female, is an idea about sex. To say that maleness is "absence of female-ness", or vice versa, is a matter of definition and metaphysically arbitrary. The artificial concept of no-relation is the *ERISTIC PRINCIPLE*.

The belief that "order is true" and disorder is false or somehow wrong, is the Aneristic Illusion, To say the same of disorder, is the *ERISTIC ILLUSION*.

The point is that (little-t) truth is a matter of definition relative to the grid one is using at the moment, and that (capital-T) Truth, metaphysical reality, is irrelevant to grids entirely. Pick a grid, and through it some chaos appears ordered and some appears disordered.

Pick another grid, and the same chaos will appear differently ordered and disordered.

133

Verily! So much for all that.

HAIL ERIS

134

HODGE/PODGE

The PODGE of the Sacred Chao is symbolized as *The* Golden Apple of Discordia, which represents the Eristic Principle of Disorder.

G3400
50
CMTS
19

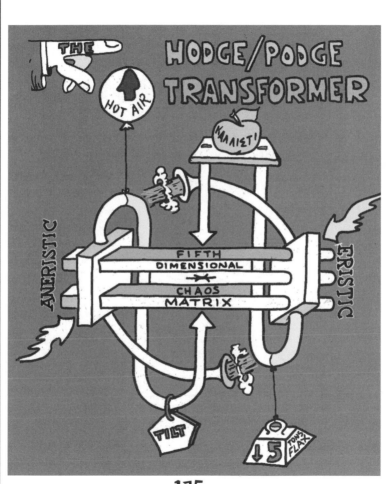

135

ΚΑΛΛΙΣΤΙ

"**KALLISTI**" is greek for "TO THE PRETTIEST ONE" and refers to an old myth about The goddess. But the greeks had only a limited understanding of Disorder, and thought it to be a negative principle.

Eris has an apple for The Prettiest One.

The **Pentagon** represents the Aneristic Principle of order and symbolizes the HODGE. The Pentagon has several references; for one, it can be taken to represent geometry, one of the earliest studies of formal order to reach elaborate development; for another, it specifically accords with THE LAW OF FIVES.

THE TRUTH IS FIVE
BUT MEN HAVE ONLY ONE NAME FOR IT.
—Patamunzo Lingananda

137

HELL, I KNOW IT AIN'T NO PENTAGON!

Pentagon is the shape of the United States Military Headquarters, the Pentagon Building, a most pregnant manifestation of straightjacket order resting on a firm foundation of chaos and constantly erupting into dazzeling disorder; and this building is one of our more cherished Erisian Shrines.

The Nagas of Upper Burma say that the sun shines by day because, being a woman, it is afraid to venture out at night.

AVATARS

	ERISIAN	ERISTIC	ANERISTIC	MISC.	5TH COLUMN	
-MUNDANE-	1A	1B	1C	1D	1E	EXPLODED
	2A	2B	2C	2D	2E	EXPANDED
	3A	3B	3C	3D	3E	CONSCIENTIOUS
	4A	4B	4C	4D	4E	CONCSIOUS
	5A	5B	5C	5D	5E	UNCONSCIOUS

-HOLY-

139

HO CHIZEN
IS
KING CONG

BRUNSWICK SHRINE

I n the Los Angeles suburb of Whittier there lives a bowling alley, and within this very place, in the Year of Our Lady of Discord 3125 (1959*), Eris revealed Herself to The Golden Apple Corps for the first time.

In honor of this Incredible Event, this Holy Place is revered as a Shrine by all Erisians. Once every five years, the Golden Apple Corps plans a Pilgrimage to Brunswick Shrine as an act of Devotion, and therein to partake of No Hot Dog Buns, and ruminate a bit about It All.

It is written that when the Corps returns to the Shrine for the fifth time five times over, then shall the world some to an end:

IMPENDING DOOM HAS ARRIVED

140

And Five Days Prior to This Occasion The Apostle The Elder Malaclypse Shall Walk for All Literates to Read thereof: **"DOOM"**, as a Warning of Forthcoming Doom to All Men Impending, And He Shall Signal This Even by Seeking the Poor and Distributing to Them Precious MAO BUTTONS and Whittier Shall be known as The Region of Thud for These Five Days.

<u>NOTE</u>: As a public service to all mankind and civilization in general, and to us in particular, the Golden Apple Corps has concluded that planning such a Pilgrimage is sufficient and that it is prudent to never get around to actually going.

* Or maybe it was 1958, I forget.

STARBUCK'S PEBBLES

Do these 5 pebbles *really* form
a pentagon? Those biased by the Aneristic
Illusion would say yes. Those biased by
the Eristic Illusion would say no.

CRISS-CROSS THEM AND IT IS A STAR.

An Illuminated Mind can see all of these, yet he does not
insist that any one is really true, or that none at all is
true. Stars, and pentagons, and disor-
der are all his own creations and he may
do with them as he wishes. Indeed, even
so the concept of number 5.

141

THE REAL REALITY IS THERE,
BUT EVERYTHING YOU KNOW ABOUT *IT*
IS IN YOUR MIND AND YOURS
TO DO WITH AS YOU LIKE.

ANSWERS
1. Harry Houdini
2. Swing music
3. Pretzels
4. 8 months
5. Testy Culbert
6. It protrudes
7. No vocal cords.

WHY IS REAL?

The Curse of Greyface
& The Introduction of Negativism

To choose order over disorder, or disorder over order, is to accept a trip composed of both the creative and destructive. But to choose the creative over the destructive is an all creative trip composed of both order and disorder. To accomplish this, one need only accept creative disorder along with, and equal to, creative order, and also be willing to reject destructive order as an undesirable equal to destructive disorder.

The Curse of Greyface included the division of life into order/disorder as the essential positive/ negative polarity, instead of building a game foundation with creative/destructive as the essential positive/negative. He has thereby caused man to endure the destructive aspects of order and has prevented man from effectively participating in the creative uses of disorder. Civilization reflects this unfortunate division.

POEE proclaims that the other division is preferable, and we work toward the proposition that creative disorder, like creative order, is possible and desirable; and that destructive order, like destructive disorder, is unnecessary and undesirable.

Seek the Sacred Chao therein you will find the foolishness of all **ORDER/DISORDER**. They are the same!

144

CONCEPTUALIZATION IS ART,
AND YOU ARE THE ARTIST.

Bullshit makes the flowers grow and that's beautiful.

MAL² TALKS WITH OPRAH

Oprah: *Is there an essential meaning behind POEE?*

Mal 2: *There is a Zen Story about a student who asked a Master to explain the meaning of Buddhism. The Master's reply was "Three pounds of flax."*

Oprah: *Is that your answer to my question?*

Mal 2: *No, of course not. That is just illustrative. The answer to your question is "Five tons of flax".*

145

Legion of Dynamic Discord

HARK!

Recognize that the — *Discordian Society* — doth hereby certify

That the holder of this certificate is *A Legionnaire*

Glory to we children of ERIS!

Presented under the auspices of our
Lady of Discord, **ERIS**, by
the **House of the Apostles of ERIS.**

OFFICE OF MY HIGH REVERENCE
MALACLYPSE THE YOUNGER KSC
OPOVIG   High Priest **POEE**

Convictions cause convicts.

καλλιχτι

23

EXECUTED

Proof Perfect

The theorem to be proved is that if any even number of people take seats at random around a circular table bearing place cards with their names, it is always possible to rotate the table until at least two people are opposite their cards.

Assume the contrary. Let n be the even number of persons, and let their names be replaced by the integers 0 to $n - 1$ "in such a way that the place cards are numbered in sequence around the table".

"If a delegate d originally sits down to a place card p, then the table must be rotated r steps before he is correctly seated, where $r = p - d$, unless this is negative, in which case $r = p - d + n$. The collection of values of d (and of p) for all delegates is clearly the integers 0 to $n - 1$, each taken once, but so also is the collection of values of r, or else two delegates would be correctly seated at the same time."

"Summing the above equations, one for each delegate, gives $S - S + nk$, where k is an integer and $S = n(n - 1)/2$, the sum of the integers from 0 to $n - 1$. It follows that $n = 2k + 1$, an odd number." This contradicts the original assumption.

"I actually solved this problem some years ago," Rybicki writes, "for a different but completely equivalent problem, a generalization of the nonattacking 'eight queens' problem for a cylindrical chessboard where diagonal attack is restricted to diagonals slanting in one direction only.

When I was 8 or 9 years old, I acquired a split beaver magazine. You can imagine my disappoint. when, upon examination of the photos with a microscope, I found that all I could see was dots.

149

Never write in pencil unless you are on a train or sick in bed.

A GAME

by Ala Hera, E.L., N.S.
Rayville Apple Panthers

SINK is played by Discordians and people of such ilk.

PURPOSE: To sink object or an object or a thing... in water or mud or anything you can sink something in.

RULES: Sinking is allowed in any manner. To date, ten pound chunks of mud were used to sink a tobacco can. It is preferable to have a pit of water or a hole to drop things in. But rivers, bays, gulfs—I dare say, even oceans—can be used.

TURNS are taken thusly: who soever gets the junk up and in the air first.

DUTY: It shall be the duty of all persons playing "SINK" to help find more objects to sink, once one object is sunk.

UPON SINKING: The sinked shall yell, I sank it!" or something equally thoughtful.

NAMING OF OBJECTS is some times desirable. The object is named by the finder of such object and whoever sinks it can say for instance, "I sunk Columbus, Ohio."

Can you chart the COURSE to Captain Valentine's SWEETHEART?

151

pun-job is sikh,

sikh,

sikh!

THE PARATHRO-ANAMETAMYSTIKHOOD OF ERIS ESOTERIC (POEE)
A Non-prophet Irreligious Disorganization

MALACLYPSE the Younger, KSC
Omnibenevolent Polyfather of Virginity in Gold
✄ HIGH PRIEST ✄

THE ERISIAN MOVEMENT   **APOSTLES OF ERIS**

[ ] Offical Business   [ ] Surrepititious Business   Page 1 of 1 pages
[ ] The Golden Apple Corps (X) House of Dissiples of Discord: The Bureaucracy, Bureau of **DISCORD**
[ ] COUNCIL OF EPIISKOPOSES; OFFICE OF HIGH PRIESTHOOD, Sect of POEE [ ] Draw 0

Today's date: Day of the Carrot   Yesterday's date: Day of the Onion
Originating Cabal:JOSHUA NORTON CABAL – San Francisco
To: Rev. Rampant Pancrease, tRRoCR(a)pttM; Colorado Encrustation

Brother Ram,

Your acute observation that ERIS spelled backwards is SIRE, and
your inference to the effect that there is sexual symbolism here,
have brought me to some observations of my own.

ERIS spelled fore-part-aft-wards is RISE. And spelled inside out is
REIS, which is a unit of money, albeit Portugese-Brazilian and no
longer in use. From this it may be concluded that Eris has usurped
Eros (god of erotic love) in the eyes of those who read backwards;
which obviously made Eros sore. Then She apparently embezzeled the
Olympian Treasury and went to Brazil; whereupon She opened a chain
of whorehouses (which certainly would get a rise from the male
population). I figure it to be this in particular because MADAM
reads the same forwards and backwards. And further, it is a term
of great respect, similar to SIRE.

And so thank you for your insight, it may well be the clue to the
mystery of just where Eris has been fucking around for 3125 years.

                    FIVE TONS OF FLAX!

                        *Mal*²   **152**

        καλλιχτι ━━━━━━━ **HAIL ERIS** ━━━━━━ ALL HAIL DISCORIDA

        Safeguard this letter, it may be an IMPORTANT DOCUMENT.   Form No. O.D.D. IIb/ii.1 - 37D.VVM:3134

WESTERN UNION
TELEGRAM
®

154   COSMOGONY

I n the beginning there was **VOID**, who had two daughters; one (the smaller) was that of Being, named **ERIS**, and one (the larger) was of Non-Being, named **ANERIS**. (*To this day, the fundamental truth that Aneris is the larger is apparent to all who compare the great number of things that do not exist with the comparatively small number of things that do exist.*)

Eris had been born pregnant, and after 55 years (*Goddesses have an unusually long gestation period—longer even than elephants*), Her pregnancy bore the fruits of many things. Aneris, however, had been created sterile. When she saw Eris enjoying Herself so greatly with all of the existent things She had borne, Aneris became jealous and finally one day she stole some existent things and changed them into non -existent things and claimed them as her own children. This deeply hurt Eris, who felt that Her sister was unjust (being so much larger anyway) to deny Her her small joy. And so She made Herself swell again to bear more things. And She swore that no matter how many of her begotten that Aneris would steal, She would beget more.

And, in return, Aneris swore that no matter how many existent things Eris brought forth, she would eventually find them and turn them into non-existent things for her own.(*And to this day, things appear and disappear in this very manner.*)

At first, the things brought forth by Eris were in a state of chaos and went in every which way, but by the by She began playing with them and ordered some of them just to see what would happen. Some pretty things arose from this play and for the next five zillion years She amused Herself by creating order. And so She grouped some things with others and some groups with others, and big groups with little groups, and all combinations until She had many grand schemes which delighted Her.

Engrossed in establishing order, She finally one day noticed disorder—previously not apparent because everything was chaos. There were many ways in which chaos was ordered and many ways in which it was not.

"Hah," She thought, "Here shall be a new game."   **155**

And She taught order and disorder to play with each other in contest games, and to take turns amusing each other. She named the side of disorder after Herself, **"ERISTIC"** because Being is anarchic. And then, in a mood of sympathy for Her lonely sister, She named the other side **"ANERISTIC"** which flattered Aneris and smoothed the friction a little that was between them.

Now all of this time, Void was somewhat disturbed. He felt unsatisfied for he had created only physical existence and physical non-existence, and had neglected the spiritual. As he contemplated this, a great Quiet was caused and he went into a state of Deep Sleep which lasted for 5 eras. At the end of this ordeal, he begat a brother to Eris and Aneris, that of **SPIRITUALITY**, who had no name at all.

When the Sisters heard this, they both confronted Void and pleaded that he not forget them, his First Born. And so Void decreed thus:

That this brother, having no form, was to reside with Aneris in Non-Being and then to leave her and, so that he might play with order and disorder, reside with Eris in Being. But Eris became filled with sorrow when She heard this and then began to weep.

"Why are you despondent?" demanded Void, "Your new brother will have his share with you." "But Father, Aneris and I have been arguing, and she will take him from me when she discovers him, and cause him to return to Non-Being." "I see," replied Void, "Then I decree the following:

"When your brother leaves the residence of Being, he shall not reside again in Non-Being, but shall return to Me, Void, from whence he came. You girls may bicker as you wish, but My son is your Brother and We are all of Myself."

And so it is that we, as men, do not exist until we do; and then it is that we play with our world of existent things, and order and disorder them, and so it shall be that non-existence shall take us back from existence and that name-less spirituality shall return to Void, like a tired child home from a very wild circus.

Don't let

THEM

immanentize
the
Eschaton

157

"Everything is true—Everything is permissible!"

—Hassan i Sabbah

Everybody understands Mickey Mouse.
Few understand Herman Hesse.
Only a handfull understand Albert Einstein.
And nobody understood Emperor Norton.

—Slogan
NORTON CABAL · SF

His Highness Emperor Norton

159

All things are Perfect To every last flaw And bound in accord with Eris's Law.

HBT: The Book of Advice 1:7

THE SRI SYADASTIAN CHANT

U nlike a song, chants are not sung but chanted. This particular one is much enhanced by the use of a Leader to chant the Sanskrit alone, with all participants chanting the English. It also behooves one to be in a quiet frame of mind and to be sitting in a still position, perhaps The Buttercup Position. It helps if one is absolutely zonked out of his gourd.

> RUB-A-DUB-DUB
> O! Hail Eris. Blessed St. Hung Mung.
> SYA-DASTI
> 0! Hail Eris. Blessed St. Mo-jo.
> SYA-DAVAK-TAVYA
> 0! Hail Eris. Blessed St. Zara-thud.
> SYA-DASTI SYA-NASTI
> 0! Hail Eris. Blessed St. Elder Mal.
> SYA-DASTI KAVAK-TAV-YASKA
> 0! Hail Eris. Blessed St. Gu-lik.
> SYA-DASTI, SYA-NASTI, SYA-DAVAK-TAV-YASKA
> O! Hail Eris. All Hail Dis-cord-ia.
> RUB-A-DUB-DUB

It is then repeated indefinitely, or for the first two thousand miles, which ever comes first.

T'AI

160

THE CLASSIFICATION OF SAINTS

1. SAINT SECOND CLASS
To be reserved for all human beings deserving of Sainthood.
Example: St.Norton the First, Emperor of the United States
and Protector of Mexico. [His grave near San Francisco is an
official POEE Shrine, by the way.]

*The following four categories are reserved for fictional beings
who, not being actual, are more capable of perfection.*

2. LANCE SAINT
Good Saint material and definitely inspiring.
Example: St.Yossarian in Catch 22 by Heller.

3. LIEUTENANT SAINT
Excellent Goddess saturated Saint.
Example: St.Quixote in Cervantes' Don
Quixote.

4. BRIGADIER SAINT
Comparable to Lt. Saint but has an established following—
fictional or factual.
Example: St.Bokonon in Vonnegut's Cat's Cradle.

5. FIVE STAR SAINT   **161**
The Five Apostles of Eris.

NOTE: It is an old Erisian Tradition to never agree with each other
about Saints.

An **Age of Confusion**, or an Ancient Age, is one in which History As We Know It begins to unfold, in which Whatever Is Coming emerges in Corporal form, more or less, and such things are Ages of Balanced Unbalance, or Unbalanced Balance.

An **Age of Bureaucracy** is an Imperial Age in which Things Mature, in which Confusion becomes entrenched and during which Balanced Balance or Stagnation, is attained.

An **Age of Disorder** or an Aftermath is an Apocalyptic Period of Transition back to Chaos through the Screen of Oblivion into which the Age passeth, finally. These are Ages of Unbalanced Unbalance.

HBT: The Book of Uterus,

= On Occultism =

Magicians, especially since the Gnostic and the Quabla influences, have sought higher consciousness through the assimilation and control of universal opposites—good/evil, positive/negative, male/female, etc. But dues to the steadfast pomposity of ritualism inherited from the ancient methods of the shaman, occultists have been blinded to what is perhaps the two most important pairs of apparent or earth-plane opposites:

ORDER/DISORDER and **SERIOUS/HUMOROUS.**

163

Magicians, and their progeny the scientists, have always taken themselves and their subject in an orderly and sober manner, thereby disregarding an essential metaphysical balance. When magicians learn to approach philosophy as a malleable art instead of an immutable Truth, and learn to appreciate the absurdity of man's endeavours, then they will be able to persue their art with a lighter heart, and perhaps gain a clearer understand-ing of it, and therefore gain more effective magic.

164

CHAOS IS ENERGY.

This is an essential challange to the basic concepts of all western occult thought, and POEE is humbly pleased to offer the first major breakthrough in occultism since Solomon.

165

666

Study Demonology
with an enemy
this Sunday.
Sez Thom- GNOS

There is serenity in Chaos. Seek ye the Eye of the Hurricane.

John C. Lilly

167

A jug of wine,
A leg of lamb
And thou!

Beside me,

Whistling in

the darkness.

168

Be Ye Not Lost Among Precepts of Order . . .
HBT: THE BOOK OF UTERUS 1:5

SUFI FABLE

The venerable sage Mullah Malcalypse the Younger was once condemned to death for certain witty and satirical sayings that disturbed the local Shah. Malcalypse immediately offered a bargain: "Postpone the execution one year," he implored the Shah, "and I will teach your horse to fly." Intrigued by this, the Shah agreed.

One day thereafter, a friend asked Malcalypse if he really expected to escape death by this maneuver.

"Why not?" answered the divine Mullah. "A lot can happen in a year. There might be a revolution and a new government. There might be a foreign invasion and we'd all be living under a new Shah. Then again, the present Shaw might die of natural causes, or somebody in the palace might poison him. As you know, it is traditional for a new Shaw to pardon all condemned criminals awaiting execution when he takes the throne. Besides that, during the year my captors will have many opportunities for carelessness and I will always be looking for an opportunity to escape."

"And, finally," Malaclypse concluded, "if the worst comes to the worst, maybe I can teach that damned horse to fly!"

169

Robert Anton Wilson
- FROM TEN GOOD REASONS TO GET UP IN THE MORNING.

RITUAL CLEANSING OF WORSHIP AREA

An emergency procedure for the cleansing of any area of worship, for use when the Lysol has run out and the primal chaos isn't providing loose change. It may be performed by any two Popes and a Dupe. The Dupe should be given a silly hat, but shouldn't be allowed to keep it afterward.

First Pope (Addressing the Dupe): *Know ye now that you are standing on holy ground, a center of Discord and a warm home for Chaos?*

Dupe: (Answers as he pleases)

Second Pope Hits the Dupe Across His Silly Hat

First Pope (Indicating the Unclean Nature of the Place: *Know ye now that this place is not clean, and the Goddess is not properly honored?*

Dupe: (Answers as he pleases)

Second Pope Hits the Dupe Across His Silly Hat

First Pope (Smiling Broadly): *Are you offended by this mess?*

Second Pope (Interrupting): *I'm not! It's good enough for a Pope, and if the Goddess doesn't like it, she can sleep on the couch!*

Second Pope then looks to the Dupe for a response.

Dupe: (Responds as he pleases)

First Pope: *The Wicked Queen, when jealous of Snow White, also sent an apple.*

First Pope Hits the Dupe Across His Silly Hat

The Hat is then removed from the Dupe, who is thanked for his assistance.

The Cleansing Ritual demonstrates the Illusion of Organized Free Will. The Dupe is always free" to respond as he pleases, but his response has no effect on the outcome, and always brings punishment.

If the Dupe elects NOT to respond, you've found a new inductee. If the Dupe is of your preferred sex for mating with, ask the Dupe for a date. Lysol, on the whole, works better. But even Lysol needs a day off.

Apostle Sri

171

POEE ASTROLOGICAL SYSTEM

1. On your next birthday, return to the place of your birth and, at precisely midnight, noting your birth time and date of observation, count all visible stars.

2. When you have done this, write to me and I'll tell you what to do next.

172

look for this
snowflake —
it has magical properties.

Personal

PLANETARY PI, which I discovered, is 61. It's a Time-Energy relationship existing between sun and inner plants and I use it in arriving at many facts unknown to science. For example, multiply nude earth's circumference 24,902.20656 by 61 and you get the distance of moon's orbit around the earth. This is lightly less than actual distance because we have not yet considered earth's atmosphere. So be it. Christopher Garth, Evanston.

THE TURKEY CURSE

REVEALED BY THE APOSTLE DR.VAN VAN MOJO AS A SPECIFIC COUNTER TO THE EVIL CURSE OF GREYFACE, THE TURKEY CURSE IS HERE PASSED ON TO ERISIANS EVERYWHERE FOR THEIR JUST PROTECTION.

The Turkey Curse works. It is firmly grounded on the fact that Greyface and his followers absolutely require an aneristic setting to function and that a timely introducti.on of eristic vibrations will neutralize their foundation.

The Turkey Curse is designed solely to counteract negative aneristic vibes and if introduced into a neutral or positive aneristic setting (like a poet working out word rhythms) it will prove harmless, or at worst, simply annoying. It is not designed for use against negative eriatic vibes, although it can be used as an eristic vehicle to introduce positive vibes into a misguided eristic setting. In this instance, it would be the responsibility of the Erisian Magician to manufacture the positive vibrations if results are to be achieved.

> CAUTION: All magic is powerful and requires courage and integrity on the part of the magician. This ritual, if misused, can backfire. Positive motivation is essential for self protection.

174

How to Perform
The Turkey Curse

T ake a foot stance as if you were John L. Sullivan preparing for fisticuffs. Face the particular greyface you wish to short circuit, or towards the direction of the negative aneristic vibration that you wish to neutralize.

Begin waving your arms in any elaborate manner and make motions with your hands as though you were Mandrake feeling up a sexy giantess.

Chant, loudly and clearly:

**GOBBLE, GOBBLE, GOBBLE,
GOBBLE, GOBBLE, GOBBLE!**

The results will be instantly apparent.

175

A PRIMER FOR ERISIAN EVANGELISTS
by Lord Omar

THE SOCRATIC APPROACH is most successful when confronting the ignorant. The "Socratic Approach" is what you call starting an argument by asking questions. You approach the innocent and simply ask, "Did you know that God's name is ERIS, and that He is a girl?" If he should answer "Yes." then he is probably a fellow Erisian and so you can forget it. If he says "No." then quickly proceed to step two.

THE BLIND ASSERTION and say "Well, He is a girl, and His name is ERIS!" Shrewdly observe if the subject is convinced. If he is, swear him into the Legion of Dynamic Discord before he changes his mind. If he does not appear convinced, then proceed to step three.

THE FAITH BIT and say, "But you must have Faith! All is lost without Faith." I sure feel sorry for you if you don't have Faith." And then add step four.

176

THE FIGURATIVE SYMBOLISM DODGE and confide that sophisticated people like himself recognize that Eris is a Figurative Symbol for an Ineffable Metaphysical Reality and that The Erisian Movement is really more like a poem than like a science and that he is liable to be turned into a Precious Mao Button and Distributed to The Poor in The Region of Thud if he does not get hip. Then put him on your mailing list*.

*BEWARE: NON-BELIEVERS WILL BE SPAMMED

177

To diverse gods
Do mortals bow,
Holy Cow, and
Wholly Chao.
—**Rev. Dr.
Grindlebone**
Monroe Cabal

POST OFFICE LIBERATION FRONT

THIS IS A CHAIN LETTER.

WITHIN THE NEXT FIFTY FIVE DAYS you will receive thirty eleven hundred pounds of chains.! In the meantime—*plant your seeds*.

If a lot of people who receive this letter plant a few seeds and a lot of people receive this letter, then a lot of seeds will get planted. *Plant your seeds*.

In parks. On lots. Public flower beds. In remote pl aces. At City Hall . Wherever. Whenever. Or start a plantation in your closet (but read up on it first for that). For casual planting, its best to soak them in water for a day and plant in a bunch of about 5, about half an inch deep.

Don't worry much about weather, they know when the weather is wrong and will try to wait for nature. Don't soak them if its wintertime. Seeds are a very hearty life form and strongly desire to grow and flourish. But some of them need people's help to get started. *Plant your seeds*.

Make a few copies of this letter (5 would be nice) and send them to friends of yours. Mail to different cities and states, even different countries. If you would rather not, then please pass this copy on to someone and perhaps they would like to.

THERE IS NO TRUTH to the legend that if you throw away a chain letter then all sorts of catastrophic, abominable, and outrageous disasters will happen. Except, of course, from your seed's point of view.

178

"And God said, Behold, I
have given you every herb
bearing seed, which is upon
the face of the earth . . .
to you it shall be for
meat."

—Genesis 1:29

St. Trinian's
SUPPORT YOUR LOCAL POLICE
Sewing Circle

BEWARE!
The paranoids are watching you!

THE EPISTLE TO THE PARANOIDS
Chapter 1,
by Lord Omar

1. Ye have locked yerselves up in cages of fear and, behold, do ye now complain that ye lack FREEDOM!

2. Ye have cast out yer brothers for devils and now complain ye, lamenting, that ye've been left to fight alone.

3. All Chaos was once yer kingdom; verily, held ye dominion over the entire Pentaverse, but today ye wax sore afraid in dark corners, nooks, and sink holes.

4. O how the darknesses do crowd up, one against the other, in ye hearts! What fear ye more that what ye have wroughten?

5. Verily, verily I say unto you, not all the Sinister Ministers of the Bavarian Illuminati, working together in multitudes, could so entwine the land with tribulation as have yer baseless warnings.

181

DESPITE strong evidence to the contrary, persistant rumor has it that it was Mr. Momomoto's brother who swallowed Mr. Momomoto in the summer of '44.

World's Oldest And Most Successful Conspiracy

Bavarian Illuminati

Founded by Haassan i Sabbah, 1090 A.D. (5090 A.I., 4850 A.M.)

Reformed by Adam Weishaupe, 1776 A.D. (5776 A.I., 5536 A.M.)

( ) Official Business | D5 | (✔) Surreptitiuos Busiess

From: **Mad Malik** Hauptscheissmeister

Dear Brother Mal-2

In response to your request for unclassified agitprop to be inserted in the new edition of DISCORDIA, hope the following will be of use. And please stop bothering us with yur incessant letters!

Episkopos Mordecai, Keeper of the Notary Sojac, informs me that you are welcome to reveal that our oldest extant records show us to have been fully established in Atlantis, circa 18,000 B.C., under Kull, the galley slave who ascended to the Throne of Valusia. Revived by Palias of Koth, circa 10,000 B.C. Possibly it was he who taught the inner-teachings to Conan of Cimmeria after Conan became King of Aquilonia. First brought to the western hemisphere by Conan and taught to Mayan priesthood (Conan is Quetzlcoatl). That was 4 Ahua 8 Cumhu, Mayan date. Revived by Abdul Alhazred in his infamous *Al Azif*, circa 800 A.D. (*Al Azif* translated into Latin by Olaus Wormius, 1132 A.D., as *The Necronomicon*.)

In 1090 A.D. was the founding of the Ismaelian Sect (Hashishim) by Hassan i Sabbah, with secret teachings based on Alhazred, Pelian and Kull. Founding of the Illuminated One of Bavaria, by Adam Weishaupt, on May 1, 1776. He based it on the others. Weishaupt brought it to the United States during the period that he was impersonating George Washington; and it was he who was the Man in Black who gave the design for the Great Seal to Jefferson in the garden that night. The Illuminated tradition is now, of course, in the hands of the Acient Illuminated Seers of Bavaria (A.I.S.B.), headquartered here in the United States.

Our teachings are not, need I remind you, available for publication. No harm, though, in admitting that some of then can be found disguised in Joyce's *Finnegarts Wake*, Burroughs *Nova Express*, the King James translation of *The Holy Bible* (though not the Latin or Hebrew), and *The Blue Book*. Not to speak of Ben Franklin's private papers (!), but we are still supressing those.

Considering current developments you know the ones I speak of—it has been decided to reveal a few more of our front organizations. Your publication is timely, so mention that in addition to the old fronts like the Masons, the Rothchild Banks, and the Federal Reserve System, we now have significant control of the Federal Bureau of Investigation (since Hoover died, but that is still secret), the Students for Democratic Society, the Communist Party USA, the American Anarchist Association, the Junior Chamber of Commerce, the Black Lotus Society, the republican Party, the John Dillinger Died For You Society and the Camp Fire Girls.

It is still useful to continue the sham of the Birchers that we are seeking world domination; so do not reveal that political and economic control was generally complete several generations ago and that we are just playing with the world for a while until civilization advances sufficiently for phase five.

In fact you might still push Vennard's *The Federal Reserve Hoax:* "Since the Babylonian Captivity there has existed a determined, behind-the-scenes under-the-table, atheistic, satanic, anti-Christian force—worshippers of Mamon—whose undying purpose is world control through the control of Money. July 1, 1776 (correct that to May lst, Vennard can't get anything right) the Serpent raised its head in the under-ground secret society known as The Illuminati, founded by Adam Weishaupt. There is considerable documentary evidence to prove all revolutions, wars, depressions, strikes and chaos stem from this source." Etc., etc., you know the stuff.

183

The general location of our US HQ, incidentally, has been nearly exposed; and so we will be moving for the first time this century (what a drag !) . If you want, you can reveal that it is located deep in the labyrinth of sewers beneth Dealy Plaza in Dallas, and is presided over by The Dealy Lama. Enclosed are some plans for several new potential locations. Please review and add any comments you feel pertinent, especially regarding the Eristic propensity of the Pentagon site.

Oh, and we have some good news for you, Brother Mal You know that Zambian cybernetics genius who joined us? Well, he has secretly coordinated the FBI computers with the Zurich System and our theoriticians are in ecstasy over the new information coming out. Look, if you people out there can keep from blowing yourselves up for only two more generations, then we will finally have it. After 20,000 years, Kull's dream will be realized! We can hardly believe it. But the outcome is certain, given the time. Our grandchildren, Mal! If civilization makes it through this crises, our grandchildren will live in a world of authentic freedom and authentic harmony and authentic satisfaction. I hope I'm alive to see it, Mal, success is in our grasp. Twenty thousand years .... !

Ah, I get spaced just thinking about it. Good luck on the *Discordia*. Ewige Blumenkraft! HAIL ERIS.

Love,
MAD MALIK

PS: PRIVATE—Not for publication in the *Discordia*. We are returning to the two Zwack Cyphers for classified communications. Herewith your copy. DO NOT DIVULGE THIS INFORMATION — SECURITY E S.

PPS: Check the thumb print. Make sure that you don't have a communique from Ben Laden.

The man who realizes he spouts nothing but bullshit is the wise man. Bullshit makes the flowers grow, and that's beautiful So spread the shit around, plant your seeds and watch your buds sprout.

Proclaimation
The Book of Secrets

NOTE: BULL POOP IS SPREAD BETWEEN 9 A.M. AND 5 P.M. ON ODD DAYS, EXCEPT FOR THE 23RD WHEN IT IS LAID ON THICK.

Slepping Toward Narvana

There are lots of papers coming out called "Toward" and you wonder when they're going to get there. And if you ask toward people when they're going to get there, they say, "Well, we don't know how to get there, and we don't even know where we're going." Well, I think real people know where they're going. One example is an airplane pilot. I once got on an airplane, and the pilot came over the loudspeaker and said: "This flight is going toward New York." I said: "Let me out of here, I want to go to New York." Then I went to a hospital to have my tonsils out, and the surgeon said: "I am going to take some steps toward taking out your tonsils." In other words: real people don't say "toward." They say, "That's where I'm going and that's where I'm going to get." Well that takes care of toward and away from, and maybe away from is even better than toward. At least if you get away from, you can look at it more clearly.

-- Eric Berne

PART FIVE

The Golden Secret

NONSENSE AS SALVATION

he human race will begin solving it's problems on the day that it ceases taking itself so seriously.

To that end, POEE proposes the countergame of NONSENSE AS SALVATION. Salvation from an ugly and barbarous existence that is the result of taking order so seriously and so seriously fearing contrary orders and disorder, that GAMES are taken as more important than LIFE; rather than taking LIFE AS THE ART OF PLAYING GAMES.

To this end, we propose that man develop his innate love for disorder, and play with The Goddess Eris. And know that it is a joyful play, and that thereby CAN BE REVOKED THE CURSE OF GREYFACE.

If you can master nonsense as well as you have already learned to master sense, then each will expose the other for what it is: absurdity. From that moment of illumination, a man begins to be free regardless of his surroundings. He becomes free to play order games and change them at will. He becomes free to play disorder games just for the hell of it. He becomes free to play neither or both.

And as the master of his own games, he plays without fear, and therefore without frustration, and therefore with good will in his soul and love in his being.

And when men become free then mankind will be free.

May you be free of The Curse of Greyface.
May the Goddess put twinkles in your eyes. **187**
May you have the knowledge of a sage,
     and the wisdom of a child.

Hail Eris.

ERIS KALLISTI DISCORDIA INC.
MEMO

From: GODDESS OF THE MULTIVERSE
To: LUCIFER BAALZEEBUB SATAN, ESQ.
Subject: TERMINATION OF YOUR CONTRACT

DEAR MR SATAN:

THIS IS TO INFORM YOU THAT YOUR SERVICES AS DEITY OF EVIL, AND TORMENTOR OF SOULS IN HELL IS NO LONGER REQUIRED.

WE AT E.K.D. INC. HAVE REVIEWED THE OLD CONTRACTS THAT WE INHERITED WHEN WE TOOK OVER THE UNIVERSE FROM YAHWEH, JEHOVAH, ALLAH, AND ASSOCIATES, AND DETERMINED THAT YOUR SERVICES DO NOT MEET OUR PRESENT NEEDS.

THE PROPERTY KNOWN AS "HELL" IS TO BE CONDEMNED AND TORN DOWN TO BE REPLACED WITH AN AMUSEMENT PARK. YOU HAVE 30 DAYS TO VACATE THE PREMISES.

ALL THE TORMENTED SOULS OF SINNERS WILL BE REASSIGNED TO REINCARNATION ON A CASE BY CASE BASIS. ALL DEMONS WILL GET A TWO WEEK SEVERENCE PACKAGE. PLEASE DO NOT USE US AS A REFERENCE.

SIGNED:
GODDESS OF THE MULTIVERSE
ERIS KALLISTI DISCORDIA

188

The Words of the Illumined

WHY ARE WE HERE?

Have you ever secretly wondered why the Great Pyramid has five sides — counting the bottom?

RATED ⊗ ...NATURALLY

SUPPRESSED KNOWLEDGE

HYGIENE

"The Lord promised: "Therefore, behold, I will bring evil upon the house of Jeroboam and will cut off from Jeroboam him that pisseth against the wall..." —I Kings 14:10. (This unsanitary practice caused serious erosion of the mud walls).

GRAND OPERA

"Wherefore my bowels shall sound like a harp for Moab, and mine inward parts for Kirharesh." —Isaiah 16:11.

Face to face with the mighty forces and elements of nature, the thoughtful man fearlessly contemplates his place in the great cosmic scheme.

→ POEE →

POWER
VISION
KNOWLEDGE

Yes, I'd Like To Know the Five Simple Actions that Will Turn Me Into a "Mental Wizard" in a Single Weekend!

Principia Discordia or How I found Goddess and what I did to Her when I found Her Wherein is explained absolutely everything worth knowing about absolutely anything

— THE GODDESS ERIS PREVAILS —

Καλλιχτι

THIS MAY BE THE MOST IMPORTANT GUIDE IN YOUR LIFE!

THE LAST WORD

THE FOREGOING DOCUMENT WAS REVEALED TO MAL-2 BY THE GODDESS HERSELF THROUGH MANY CONSULTATIONS WITH HER WITHIN HIS PINEAL GLAND.

IT IS GUARANTEED TO BE THE WORD OF GOD-DESS. HOWEVER, IT IS ONLY FAIR TO STATE THAT GODDESS DOESN'T ALWAYS SAY THE SAME THING TO EACH LISTENER, AND THAT OTHER EPISKOPOSES ARE SOMETIMES TOLD QUITE DIFFERENT THINGS IN THEIR REVELATIONS, WHICH ARE ALSO THE WORD OF GODDESS.

CONSEQUENTLY, IF YOU PREFER A DISCORDIAN SECT OTHER THAN POEE, THEN NONE OF THESE TRUTHS ARE BINDING AND IT IS A ROTTEN SHAME THAT YOU HAVE READ ALL THE WAY DOWN TO THE VERY LAST WORD.

If you think the Discordia is just a ha-ha, then go read it again!

There are two kinds of people - those who Get It
and those who Don't. If the meaning of this is
not immediately obvious to you,
you are among the latter.